My
Good
Side

My Good Side

A Memoir

SCHEANA SHAY

GRAND
CENTRAL

New York   Boston

Grand Central Publishing
Hachette Book Group
1290 Avenue of the Americas, New York, NY 10104
grandcentralpublishing.com
@grandcentralpub

First Edition: July 2025

Grand Central Publishing is a division of Hachette Book Group, Inc.
The Grand Central Publishing name and logo is a registered trademark of Hachette Book Group, Inc.

The publisher is not responsible for websites (or their content) that are not owned by the publisher.

The Hachette Speakers Bureau provides a wide range of authors for speaking events. To find out more, go to hachettespeakersbureau.com or email HachetteSpeakers@hbgusa.com.

Grand Central Publishing books may be purchased in bulk for business, educational, or promotional use. For information, please contact your local bookseller or the Hachette Book Group Special Markets Department at special.markets@hbgusa.com.

Print book interior design by Jeff Stiefel

Unless otherwise noted, all photos are courtesy of the author.

Library of Congress Cataloging-in-Publication Data

Names: Shay, Scheana, 1985- author
Title: My good side : a memoir / Scheana Shay.
Description: First edition. | New York : Grand Central Publishing, 2025.
Identifiers: LCCN 2025004032 | ISBN 9781538773352 hardcover | ISBN 9781538773376 ebook
Subjects: LCSH: Shay, Scheana, 1985- | Women television personalities—United States—Biography | Vanderpump rules (Television program) | LCGFT: Autobiographies
Classification: LCC PN1992.4.S46 A3 2025 | DDC 791.4502/8092—dc23/eng/20250502
LC record available at https://lccn.loc.gov/2025004032

ISBNs: 978-1-5387-7335-2 (hardcover), 978-1-5387-7337-6 (ebook), 978-1-5387-7559-2 (signed edition), 978-1-5387-7558-5 (B&N signed edition)

Printed in the United States of America

LSC-C

Printing 1, 2025

*For those who have felt limited or defined
by the scars and scarlet letters of their past.
And for those who saw past mine,
supported me along my journey,
or are here for the first time.*

CONTENTS

CONTENTS

My
Good
Side

INTRODUCTION

At one point there was almost a *Vanderpump Rules* without Scheana Shay.

But there's always been a Scheana Shay without *Vanderpump Rules*—a different side of me that the world has never seen. Long before I was a reality TV star, I was little Scheana, the studious overachiever, who loved to perform onstage and played on the all-boys baseball team. I was also junior high Scheana, who got bullied at school, and teenage Scheana, who was fired from her first job for distracting the boys. Then there was college Scheana, who was the face of a lawsuit against Hooters, and early-twenties Scheana, who put the "Ho" in "Hollywood," wheeling and dealing, dating celebrities, and collecting juicy stories along the way.

Even throughout my eleven seasons on *VPR*, there was so much more to me than forty-three-minute episodes could capture. I was betrayed by those closest to me, endured a divorce, got married to a second man (twice!), suffered a miscarriage, nearly died during childbirth, and lived through a major cheating scandal among my best friends—a scandal that reverberated across the globe. I also experienced something no woman should ever have to go through with her significant other, something I haven't shared with my full inner circle, much less the whole world. Until now.

With all of this said, I'm now a mother to my beautiful daughter, Summer Moon; a mental health advocate for those who struggle with OCD; the host of a successful, award-winning podcast; and a reality TV star and actress who continues to make strides in Hollywood even as the show I'm known for comes to a close. Not to mention that some of those girls who didn't want me on *VPR* twelve years ago are women I currently call friends. I've come a long way and conquered a lot of obstacles to get to where I am.

Finally, I'm at a place in my life where I'm ready to share my story with everyone who's supported me through the years—and even those who haven't!

If you're reading this book, you've probably seen a very specific side of me: Maybe it's the twentysomething-year-old girl in the tabloids with John Mayer, or the twenty-six-year-old girl being picked on at her new serving gig. Maybe you've seen me as a loyal friend, or a bad friend, or a pick-me. Maybe you've followed my motherhood journey. Maybe you cheered for the downfall of my first marriage, or cried happy tears with me at my wedding to my second husband. Whatever side you think you know, I want to welcome you. This book will show you all sides of me (including my dreaded right angles).

I peel back the layers of the *real* Scheana Shay: a mom, a wife, a performer, an entrepreneur, and a friend—a *good* friend, might I add.

If you don't believe me, try to remember that you've only been exposed to one side of me. Now, I'm taking the narrative back. So, let me show you the rest.

1

A LEAGUE OF THEIR OWN

f there's one thing you should know about me, it's that I've never been a follower. I've always been my own person and someone who forges her own path. But I'm also a natural people pleaser, and there have been times in my life when I've felt pressure to fit in in order to survive. This contradiction has been a long-standing juggling act for me because it's nearly impossible to make strong decisions for yourself while keeping everyone else happy. So, there have been moments when I simply couldn't keep all of the balls in the air, and they came crashing down.

Still, my desire to blaze my own trail has meant that I've always had a fierce independent streak. I knew that I wanted to be able to take care of myself, and that I needed and wanted more than to stay in Azusa—the city where I grew up, in the San Gabriel Valley region of Los Angeles County.

Growing up in the shadow of LA, it's probably no surprise then that the idea of being famous was a big lure for me as a kid. I was so into Disney and Nickelodeon—I would have given anything to be one of those actresses on TV. The show *Kids Incorporated* was a personal favorite. I really admired two of the stars, Jennifer Love Hewitt and Stacy "Fergie" Ferguson. When my friends and I would reenact scenes, we'd fight over who got to be Stacy and who got to be Love. After that, I was obsessed with Britney Spears on *The Mickey Mouse Club*, and as I got a little older, I wanted to cut my hair like Lacey Chabert's on *Party of Five*. I remember being drawn to girls who had a similar look to mine, because I could actually picture myself in their roles. I loved the thought of being on set and even went to live tapings of shows when I was a kid, which was so exciting, because the energy and positive reinforcement associated with performing onstage and entertaining people were intriguing to me.

There was just some spark within me that made me sure I could be an actress one day. From a very early age, I was in all of my school plays and dance recitals. I also cheered for years and competed in Miss Hawaiian Tropic pageants. Attention, validation, and words of affirmation, which I received plenty of from my parents, were my love languages. It seemed obvious that a career in Hollywood could provide me with nearly limitless affirmation, not to mention a ticket out of Azusa.

At the same time, I really looked up to my mother and wanted to be like her. She stayed in Azusa, where she'd been raised, and started a family there, so I thought that was the way life was supposed to be. It seemed like she had everything she wanted. But I always wanted more.

It all began when my mom and my birth father, Raul, met

in Las Vegas in 1983 at a Halloween party. Raul was the emcee and several years older than my mom, which she didn't know until after they'd started seeing each other.

My mom was also dating a man named Ron. Casual dating like this wasn't unusual in the '80s, and she was only eighteen years old, so it wasn't a big deal, especially because she wasn't serious with either one of them. That is, until my mom and Raul unintentionally conceived me sometime during the 1984 Summer Olympics. I don't think having a baby or being a full-time father was really on Raul's bingo card, even though he was happy to be involved from the sidelines. While my mom hadn't intended to have a child at such a young age, she always wanted kids. And when she told Ron that she was pregnant with someone else's child, he wanted to step up and raise me with her.

On May 7, 1985, I was born. My mom was practically a baby herself but was thrilled to have a daughter. Ron, who was from the Netherlands, blond, and fair-skinned, looked nothing like me, but became my father and ultimately the man I refer to as Dad.

Raul, who was Mexican American, didn't officially meet me until I was two. He and my mom had gone to court to handle child support when I was a baby, but it wasn't until they reconnected a second time to iron out those details that he really got to interact with me. Until that point, my mother had been busy figuring out her new life as a young parent, so it was difficult for her to see how Raul would figure in.

To Raul's credit, once we did connect, he started coming to all of my big events, from my first communion and my confirmation to graduations and even some birthday parties. But he took a major step back to allow Ron to be the ever-present father I needed.

Growing up, I felt like I had to hide being half Mexican. When it was just me and my mom, it was fine. Yes, she was blond like Ron, and I had brown hair, but I had cousins with brown hair, so I didn't stand out. However, when I got a little older, after my mom married my dad, they'd be at my school events together and people would notice that I didn't look like either of them. With the two of them by my side, it really hit that I didn't fit in with the predominantly Mexican student body. It felt like my identity was in question, especially because I never wanted Ron to feel like he wasn't enough or wasn't my "real" dad. He was the best father figure I ever could have asked for.

Ron was even the one who named me. My parents didn't find out if I was a boy or a girl until my mom gave birth, but my dad said that if I was a girl, he wanted to call me Sheena, like Sheena Easton—one of the most successful recording artists in the 1980s, whom they both loved. I don't think my mom was too keen on the name at first, but when I came out with a shock of black curly hair, she knew it fit. And then it was Papa, my maternal grandfather, who suggested the spelling "Scheana." My maternal grandmother, whom I called Puna and was Polish and Russian, wanted to name me Anushka. Thank God she was overruled!

The interesting thing about my parents' relationship is that, even though they were very much together, they lived separately until I was in fifth grade, when they got married. Honestly, I'm not sure why. But my mom and I occupied a small apartment, and I'd make frequent trips to my dad's, a beautiful seven-bedroom house that he lived in with his extended family.

Our apartment complex was outside of the school zone my mom went to as a kid, so we used my grandparents' address to ensure I started kindergarten at her same elementary school, which was right behind my grandparents' home. My mom liked the fact that I would be close to my grandma in case anything happened, or if I needed a family member for any reason while she was at work.

Not only did my mom grow up in that house, but it's also where she lives now. While I appreciate that she loves Azusa, there's a part of me that wishes, one day, she'll spread her wings and leave the nest.

When I turned seven, in 1992, my mom took me to the theater to see *A League of Their Own*. My great-aunt Shirley Burkovich—one of my earliest mentors, who was around a lot when I was growing up—had played for the Rockford Peaches, the real women's baseball team that inspired the movie. Her nickname was "Hustle," and she had a speaking role in the film, which I thought was so cool. Shirley was unstoppable, both on and off the field. She pursued her passions with 110 percent effort, something I admired and try to emulate in my own life. Shirley was never one to settle for what was "just for girls," so she taught me that gender shouldn't define you.

Around the same time, I was also obsessed with making up dance routines to Paula Abdul, Wilson Phillips, and Madonna. I had all of the choreography for Paula's "Opposites Attract" and "Straight Up" down pat. And since Madonna wore number 5 in *A League of Their Own*—between her and Shirley—I was determined to play baseball and be number 5. When I told my mom about my plan, she said, "Girls don't really play baseball anymore. That's for boys. Girls play softball now." I replied, "No, I want to play baseball." As I said, I always had an independent streak!

I guess my mom recognized my passion, or at least wasn't up for an argument, so she gave me her blessing to try out for the all-boys baseball team...and I made it! I ended up playing second base for the next three years. Thankfully, the boys didn't treat me any differently, which really goes to show that, when you're a kid, the gender divide isn't so wide. I felt like I could be myself and have fun without any superficial concerns. It was all about how I performed on the field and up at bat, which was very well.

Overall, my early childhood was happy. I loved my parents, was doing well on the stage and on the field, and school was easy for me. I even ended up skipping third grade and going directly to fourth. Unfortunately, this meant that I didn't see many of my old classmates and friends anymore. Since I had excelled academically and socially up to that point, I never anticipated how hard this transition would be. But over the next few years, life at school would become more challenging than I could've imagined.

2

MEAN GIRLS

Once I started junior high, I began to feel more social pressure to fit in, so I decided it was time to elevate my look. I grew out my bangs and began shaving my legs—which, as any girl knows, are two significant milestones. I was also wearing a little more makeup, overlining my lips, and penciling in my barely there eyebrows. Don't judge! It was the style back then. I wasn't allowed to wear makeup to school, per my mom's rules, so I would lie and say I had to be at school earlier. I'd smuggle my lip liner and eyebrow pencil in my bag so I could apply them in the girls' bathroom first thing, then I would wash my face clean before I walked home. I also had the long acrylic nails. I was giving Kylie Jenner before she was a glimmer in Kris's eye.

These attempts to blend in among the largely Mexican student body didn't seem to be good enough, and I started getting targeted by bullies. My last name was Jancan, my mom's maiden name, and some people changed it to Jenkins when they referred to me. The bullies also called me Güera, which is Mexican slang for "white girl." In addition to the name-calling, I got made fun of a lot for having a white family, especially because I wasn't raised with the customs of my Hispanic heritage. Being different was basically the worst thing in the world to my mind in 1990s Azusa, so it all felt very embarrassing and hurtful. And it initiated an identity struggle within me that would last for many years, since it seemed like being myself often put me on the outside.

There was a girl—let's call her Darlene—who had a problem with me because the boy that she liked, liked me. One day at recess, her friends formed a huge circle and threw us in the middle together. They were chanting, "Fight, fight, fight!" I didn't want to fight Darlene. I didn't even know how to fight! I was particularly terrified of getting hit in the face. Thankfully, some teachers broke it up. But my mom still received a call from the school, and I got suspended, which was horrifying. I was an A student who had never been in trouble. Not to mention that I wasn't the aggressor. I was the victim.

After that, my cousin David, who was like my cool, older brother and always very protective of me, went behind my parents' back and bought me a pager. All of the other kids had one, and I thought maybe getting it would finally help me blend in. Well, that plan backfired. In the mornings before school, I started receiving pages that read "013 403" (DIE HOE) and "187," which is the cop code for murder. Around the same time, I'd also get threatening notes in class. I'll never forget one that had a hand-drawn picture of a gravestone with my name on it.

Mind you, there were a lot of gangs in my area, so in my head, these weren't exactly empty threats. I wasn't even a teenager yet, and I was afraid that I was going to be jumped on my way to or from school. At times, I was genuinely scared for my life. I didn't know if any of the bullies had siblings in gangs. I've always been a lover, not a fighter, and I wasn't equipped to properly defend myself. I felt like I had no backup.

The bullying also wasn't just at school. One time at a sleepover, the girls who I thought were my friends threatened to cut off all of my very long hair if I fell asleep. So, naturally, I stayed up all night waiting for the sun to rise until I could call my mom to pick me up.

Even though I was extremely alarmed by all the bullying, I never told my parents about it. They were in their early thirties, and we were all now living under one roof in a three-bedroom apartment. Finally, we had stability within our little nuclear family. When I was in seventh grade, my mom and dad were ready to expand it. We were so excited when my mom got pregnant, but it was short-lived. She suffered a miscarriage, which was devastating for all of us.

So, when my mom got pregnant again, I was afraid that she would lose another baby, and I wanted a sibling, a possible ally, more than anything. I tried to be on my best behavior and didn't want to rock the boat or cause any issues that might stress out my parents and harm the baby. To avoid burdening my mom, I kept the torment I was experiencing at school to myself. I thought I could handle it on my own.

Through all this time, I only had one outburst. Shortly after my mom had the miscarriage, I threw myself in our empty bathtub, and I was kicking and screaming. My mom thought it was so ridiculous that, at twelve years old, I was having a tantrum. What she didn't realize was that I was dying inside, and I didn't want to tell her. I was never suicidal, and I never considered harming myself, but I remember vividly that I would wake up in the morning and think everyone would be so much happier if I was dead. I suppose you could call that depression, although I was never diagnosed, since I believed I had to keep these feelings to myself.

I think when she lost the baby, it affected me too; it was crushing on top of everything else that was going on in school. I was a very happy only child when I was younger, but as I got a little older, I thought it would be nice to have a best friend, someone who would always stand by me and understand me. No wonder I reached a breaking point.

Thankfully, my mom's pregnancy with my sister, Cortney, was successful, and I was overjoyed at the prospect of a new addition to our family. With that said, while I never felt like Cortney was replacing me, I did realize that now my dad had a biological daughter. It had just been us for twelve years, and I was certain she'd become the star of his world. I think, subconsciously, this also made me retreat a bit into my own feelings, because I didn't want them to have any reason to worry about me. I thought if I was the perfect daughter, the perfect student, who caused no problems and didn't disappoint anyone, I wouldn't be at risk of losing any of my dad's affection. That sort of pressure is a lot for a kid.

By the end of eighth grade, I was exhausted by everything that had gone down during junior high, and I just wanted to be done with it. I'd had enough. After graduation, there was a little get-together at my friend Jennifer's house, and I told Darlene to come over so we could settle our feud once and for all. It felt like my last chance to put the drama of those years behind me before high school so I could finally find my own space within a new ecosystem. And I wanted to defend myself.

After we removed our jewelry (Azusa protocol), we went at each other like the nemeses we were. The fight felt like it lasted forever, but it was probably closer to five minutes, max. There was plenty of hair pulling, scratching, kicking, hitting, and shoving into the bushes in front of Jennifer's house. It had rained that day, adding an extra-awkward, slippery layer that made everything much more difficult. While all of this was going on, I still had my ridiculously long acrylic nails, painted white with diagonal flowers across my ring finger for graduation, and I didn't want to break them. It also made it quite challenging to make a fist.

Honestly, we probably looked like two miniature versions of the women from *The Real Housewives of Atlanta* season six reunion (ahem, Porsha Williams and Kenya Moore), even though we were only little girls clawing at each other, and not even being paid for it!

When the fight broke up, I remember tasting blood in my mouth. I later found out that I'd given Darlene a black eye (yes, that's the *only* black eye I've ever given someone, despite what Raquel Leviss claims). She got grounded for the whole summer after her parents figured out what happened, so I'd say I won not only the battle with Darlene but also the war. Check, check.

Years later, there is still a part of me that wishes I could have confided in my parents more about my struggles during middle school. Even if they couldn't have helped, it would have been nice to have a safe space to express what I was going through and to receive some support. But, while they didn't know what had transpired or the extent of the bullying I'd endured, they must have realized something was up, because they enrolled me in Bishop Amat Memorial High School—a Catholic school about twenty minutes from where we lived. The good news was that it was definitely the fresh start I desperately needed. The bad news was that there were uniforms, which included both a written dress code and about a dozen unwritten dress code rules I didn't know. That was a whole other form of education.

On day one at my new school after summer break, I showed up rocking a polo shirt, Dickies pants, and my dark lip liner, ready to make a killer first impression. By the book, I was following the dress code, but I'd made it all my own. I'd told my mom not to bother buying me any of the skirts, because the uniforms were expensive and, as an apartment manager, she didn't have a hefty income. She also had private school tuition to pay.

Of course, my luck, there was not a single other girl at the school in pants. I stuck out in all of the wrong ways, again. My lips were still overlined and my eyebrows were still plucked too thin. That day, I went home to my mom and asked her to buy me all five skirts, the button-up shirts, the matching vests, and the knee-high socks, budget be damned. I also got cute clogs, because at Bishop Amat Memorial High School the only things you could change about your uniform were the accessories and the shoes. It was all about the clogs, the skater shoes, and the book bags. I was a one-shoulder book bag girl, never a backpack, because backpacks were basic and the one-shoulder styles were trendier. (PS: Now I *love* a backpack. The one-shoulder bags are not conducive to traveling.)

Despite this rocky start, high school was an amazing time in my life. As a teenager, I was finally able to be more independent. On my sixteenth birthday, all I wanted to do was get my driver's license and a job. My mom picked me up from school and took me straight to the DMV where, of course, I passed with flying colors. Next stop, Ralph's. I was hired on the spot and started bagging groceries immediately. That job was short-lived, however, as I was fired during the three-month probationary period for being a "distraction" to the boys working up front. If you think my mom didn't call the union on that one, you'd be wrong. It all was for the best, though, because it forced me to get a new job in a new industry—restaurants. Who would've thought it would pay off with a TV show a decade later?

Around this time, I also worked at the Irwindale Speedway as a hype girl for the car races. Each girl represented a different car brand; they called me "Miss Mopar." This job led to my first SAG voucher as they were filming the movie *Biker Boyz* at the Speedway. I got to meet Kid Rock, Dante and Dion Basco, and Rick Gonzalez and was even asked to be an extra, which was my first taste of being on set. I was in love! I was only seventeen at the time, but I lied about my age so I would be seen as an adult. That lie was almost uncovered when I had one of the actors over for a little make-out session and he saw my senior photo in a frame in my room. Class of 2002. Oops! Still, we exchanged numbers, and to this day we remain friends. (He now knows my real age and it's something we look back on and laugh about.)

Another exciting high school memory was when I got to be a seat filler at the Teen Choice Awards. Phones and cameras were not allowed during the show. However, I wanted to capture a moment from this experience, so I snuck in a disposable camera taped to my inner thigh. When Usher walked by, I snapped a photo, the flash went off, and I got kicked out. Fortunately, I was able to talk my way back inside, but instead of getting to watch Nelly's performance of "Hot in Herre" from the pit, I had to watch from the nosebleeds. When I met Nelly last year at Life Is Beautiful, a music festival in Las Vegas, I recounted this story. He laughed and said that he hoped I had more fun this time. I did—and got to watch from the pit this go-around.

Hollywood experiences aside, at that age I was mostly focused on my boyfriend and friends, many of whom I'm still close with. One of those friends was Michael Shay, my now ex-husband. Shay was a football player, and I was a cheerleader. I thought Shay was so cute, and even though I had a boyfriend and he was younger than I was, I think there was always a little crush there that I never told anyone about. Flirting with him was definitely fun.

My favorite memory with Shay from this time was when I was a senior in high school and he was a sophomore. Since we lived so close together, Shay and I carpooled together every day with my best friend Adri and her little brother, who was in Shay's grade and a good friend of his. This particular day, my mom's car broke down, so Papa had to drive over to get us. When Shay and I reconnected years later, I told him I wished he'd met Papa, and he reminded me that he had. Since Papa passed away shortly after, that felt so special to me.

The only real obstacle high school brought me was that my dad and I started butting heads. He was so strict and certainly didn't approve of his fourteen-year-old daughter dating, especially the guy I had my sights set on, who was three years my senior (two grade levels), drove a Honda that looked like it was straight out of *The Fast and the Furious*, and was one of the hottest guys in school. I had crushed hard on this guy throughout my freshman year, wanting him to notice me, so I found out his class schedule and orchestrated ways to make our paths cross. At the end of that school year, my efforts paid off. He asked for my number and took me out on our first date that summer. By the start of my sophomore year, we were an item and dated from when I was aged fourteen to twenty.

My dad might have been right about the age gap, though. After my boyfriend graduated, our dynamic changed. He entered the Fire Academy, and frankly, he was kind of a dick to me, and I stopped getting the attention and validation I desired from him. This led me to cheat on him—with two different people. I didn't feel like I could leave him at the time. Deep down, I hated myself for it. Cheating made me feel gross. I knew I should have just broken up with him, and I tried many times over the later years of our relationship. However, the threats that followed my attempts to leave led me to worry he would do something drastic to himself, so I stayed.

Regardless, I ended up graduating from high school with honors. I was so relieved that my days of being mistreated by the mean, popular girls in middle school were far behind me, and I was ready to move on to college.

Of course, in less than a decade, Lisa Vanderpump would transfer me from Villa Blanca to SUR, and I'd encounter that same energy once again.

3
LEGALLY ~~BLONDE~~ *Brunette*

Before we dive deeper into all things Hollywood, I need to talk about the craziest shit that has ever happened to me in the restaurant business. And, no, I'm not talking about working at Lisa Vanderpump's establishments. It went down while I was attending Azusa Pacific University—a private evangelical research university in my hometown. It was November 2003, and I had just interviewed for a job at a Hooters location that was opening up in my area.

Like all college students, I needed money for tuition, and I had student loans. I was also way more into designer clothing and accessories at the time. I loved Coach bags and Christian Dior sunglasses, because that was what Nicole Richie wore on her reality show with Paris Hilton called *The Simple Life*. True Religion jeans, which were very expensive, were a staple for me. What can I say? The heart wants what the heart wants.

I was already employed as a server at a local country club, but being as independent as possible was my top priority, so I wanted to make more money. I enjoyed working there, even though it was a little slow. Lunch shifts were really fun because on my break I'd drive the golf carts around the course and watch some rounds. As a kid, I used to watch golf on TV with my grandfather, so I already had a passion for spectating, even though I didn't play.

The country club was also useful as a little career stepping-stone. The son of one of the members worked for MTV and we went on a few dates. Later, he introduced me to Wade Robson, a dancer and choreographer who executive-produced a show called *The Wade Robson Project* there. I got to be an extra, which fueled my Hollywood dreams even more.

Unfortunately, that was the extent of my entertainment career at the time, and I felt like I needed to take things up a notch, so I could both make more money and wear a cuter uniform. When I heard the news that a new Hooters location was opening up nearby, I was all in. The bad news was that I had no idea what I was walking into in that "job interview." The Hooters manager, Juan Aponte, seemed like a normal guy—he was a dad, in fact, which put me at ease. He asked routine questions and then requested that I return later that evening to try on the uniform. It seemed strange that I would have to come back at 6:15 p.m. for a "fitting," but he said that he was just so busy with interviews until then.

To me, it sounded like I was one step closer to getting the job. The restaurant was under construction, so all of this went down in a trailer in the parking lot. And, of course, he said he would leave the trailer while I changed. He told me to stand in a certain area while I undressed so that the construction workers who were still working outside couldn't see me. He reassured me this was for *my* benefit. Didn't I want to make sure I was comfortable in the uniform? He made it seem so normal, so I didn't allow myself to think that anything sketchy might be going on. With the trailer door closed and Juan well out of sight, I was fine with changing out of the clothes I was wearing and into the Hooters tank top and shorts.

Once Juan saw me in my uniform, I was hired on the spot. He took a photo for my job profile and said he'd be in touch when the restaurant was officially open. I was excited because being picked to work at Hooters was considered a status symbol and was another form of the validation I had sought growing up. It was kind of like landing a job at Abercrombie & Fitch, where everyone looked like a model.

Months later, my doorbell rang one afternoon, and police officers were standing on my doorstep. I hadn't heard from Juan since I was hired, so I couldn't even begin to imagine that the cops had anything to do with my interview at Hooters. It was such a shock that I didn't even register what they were showing me at first. Where did they get these grainy, black-and-white photos of me? Why was I alone in what looked like a trailer? Then, it clicked.

The officers explained that Juan was caught filming women and girls—yes, teenage *girls* still in high school, as young as seventeen. He was lying through his teeth during our interaction. There was a digital camera setup in his office, and every second I spent taking off my clothes and putting on that Hooters uniform was recorded. I was as disgusted as I was completely blindsided. It was sickening to think about, mainly because I'd never been so overtly objectified by a man.

Still, I was relieved they'd at least caught the guy. It seemed like the police had solid evidence against him, so I was ready to put the whole gross experience behind me and move on with my life.

That was until I got a call from my uncle saying he'd heard that Gloria Allred was going to be making a case against Juan, and that I should contact her office. *The* Gloria Allred—as in the legendary powerhouse attorney who'd represented Nicole Brown Simpson's family in the O. J. Simpson trial and had gone toe-to-toe with some of our country's most powerful, high-profile men who did some seriously shady shit. I was both shocked and thrilled that she was ready to take on Juan Aponte and Hooters corporate. She was looking for victims willing to tell their stories in court, and I knew I had to reach out if she needed volunteers.

During our phone call, Gloria wanted to know if I would be a voice for the women and girls who were his victims. Since I spoke clearly and with conviction about what had happened to me, she thought I could help win the case. Obviously, I wanted to do whatever I could. I was studying broadcast journalism at APU, so I figured that speaking with the media would be an amazing opportunity to apply my classroom lessons to a real-world situation. I knew I was good under pressure, and I felt confident in my ability to advocate for myself and the other victims.

The publicity for the trial ended up being enormous, as the details that came out in court were beyond disturbing. For one thing, Juan had filmed more than eighty women and girls in the janky trailer that served as his "office." It was also revealed that if the victim was wearing a black bra, he would ask that she take it off, so that the black wouldn't show through the white uniform tank top. Same went for underwear that was anything other than a nude thong. *That* is how absolutely vile this guy was. He was looking for any excuse to get women to expose themselves.

These women were just looking for a job, ready to put their best foot forward. They were simply trying to make money to support themselves, support their families, or maybe save up for college or some other goal. How he took advantage of people just looking to earn a living is so sad to think about. He tricked them just like he tricked me—with a disgusting combination of fake professionalism and bogus consideration for our safety. It makes my skin crawl, thinking about just how manipulative he was. All told, more than 180 illicit recordings were found in his apartment.

Before I knew it, I was dubbed one of "the Hooters girls." I was flown across the country to do interviews and to appear on national TV shows like *Maury*, *The Big Idea with Donny Deutsch*, and *The Early Show*. The news coverage was on CNN and all over the newspapers. I was proud to do it, proud to speak up on behalf of girls and women who'd had something so terrible happen to them, especially when I knew other women didn't feel like they could take this risk. They were camera shy, shy in general, embarrassed about what had happened to them, or felt like it was their fault. I wanted to make sure that anyone who was uncomfortable could remain out of the public eye.

Still, there was another layer to these appearances, one that complicated an already totally fucked-up situation. I'd always dreamed of being on TV. But not because of some asshole who'd taken advantage of me. I hoped it would be because of my talent as an actress, not as a victim of a sleazy crime. As disappointed as I was by the situation, I was determined to take my power back from Juan by exposing him.

I think the combination of wanting to win the case and a weird blend of sadness and shame made the whole experience kind of a blur. Honestly, there are large chunks of that part of my life I can't even remember. I wonder if it's because of the stress and mixed emotions that came with tackling the lawsuit head-on. As much as I wanted Juan to go to jail where he belonged, I was struggling with some pretty overwhelming, conflicting feelings, too. I thought I knew what I was getting into by applying for a job at Hooters, and I wanted the male attention that accompanied that. Even though I knew what Juan did was wrong, I thought, Well, I guess this is what you get for trying to work at a place that objectifies women.

Becoming one of "the Hooters girls" created a level of anxiety in my personal life that I had never experienced before. Since I was at a Christian university at the time, I lost sleep wondering if this situation would get me kicked out of school. Did I violate some sort of conduct code, just by applying to work at Hooters? And did I do it again by speaking publicly about what had happened to me? Would I still be able to graduate, or would I have to transfer to another college? Would I have to explain an expulsion or a suspension to a new school? Would this haunt me for the rest of my life? These and plenty of even uglier questions ran through my head constantly. Everywhere I went, I dreaded what people were thinking and assuming about me.

Well, it's Hooters, what did she expect?

How dumb do you have to be to agree to that sort of thing?

She should have suspected something.

What a slut.

Recalling all of these sexist questions and assumptions reminds me just how mind-blowing it is that women deal with this stuff all the time. We all know how it goes, right?

Why was she walking alone at night?

She was wearing THAT? AND she was drinking? What did she think would happen?

She probably led him on.

It's fine, he said he has daughters/nieces/aunts/a mom/etc.

It's so wrong. The worst part is that even though we won our case, it was still the exception to the rule. Legally, our success over misogynistic exploitation was an outlier. Keep in mind that this trial was years before #MeToo was in people's vocabularies. Back then, there wasn't anywhere near the level of awareness that's been raised thanks to that movement. The public discourse was focused on women's guilt and not men's culpability.

Juan Aponte was sentenced to five years in prison. The evidence against him was so overwhelming, he pleaded no contest to one count of using a minor for sex acts and three counts of eavesdropping. His victims, myself included, received some financial compensation, but honestly, how do you put a dollar amount on that kind of trauma? Another sad truth is that the vast majority of predators will never spend a day in jail. We got "justice," as I guess it's defined legally, but the rarity of that, given just how many Juan Apontes there are, goes to show how much we still have to grow as a society.

In retrospect, I wish I'd listened to my gut that day when I was trying on the uniform in the trailer. But, instead of considering that something was shady, I brushed it off and convinced myself it was normal. Why? Because I was intent on people pleasing, on not causing any waves, and I thought that resisting Juan's directive would make me seem difficult and jeopardize my opportunity to get the job.

4

THE OTHER WOMAN

On May 6, 2006, I graduated from Azusa Pacific University with a Bachelor of Arts degree in communication studies with my emphasis in broadcast journalism. I'd only applied to schools that my parents could afford or that I could get a scholarship to, which I did to APU. I loved being in Southern California—the beautiful weather, the chill vibes—and, since Azusa is thirty miles east of Hollywood, I figured I could still pursue my dream of becoming a television host, specifically an MTV VJ.

I was the only person in my family to earn a college degree, which almost didn't happen. I was so over going to school that I considered dropping out. I knew I wanted a career in entertainment, and I wanted to start as young as possible. Thankfully, I didn't. Puna wanted me to finish school and, when she died after my freshman year, my will to both honor her memory and prove myself prevailed.

Sadly, it wasn't only Puna's passing that impacted me. Papa had died in April of my senior year in high school from lung cancer. We lost Oma, my paternal grandma, three days before my high school graduation. And, then on July 4 of that same year, Opa, my paternal grandpa, died from an aortic rupture. I was so close with all of them, and they were gone within fifteen months of one another, all in their midsixties. Far too young.

A few years later, when we were twenty-three, my childhood best friend Gina—who was my only ally in junior high—passed away too, which compounded the grief I was already experiencing. Unfortunately, we went to different schools, and I imagine the bullying wouldn't have happened if I'd had her by my side. She would have kept those girls in check. Around this time I also lost my uncle Marty, my mom's older brother, who was living with us and I was extremely close to. He was murdered on New Year's Day morning walking home from the 7-Eleven around the corner from my parents' house; to this day, his case is still cold. It was a deeply depressing period in my life that I've now learned through therapy contributed to my OCD—which I still suffer from to this day. It's linked to a fear of losing people close to me, a fear that my mother also perpetuated, unintentionally.

There was this song my mom would sing to me every night when I was a kid. It was called "You and Me Against the World," by Helen Reddy, and there were lyrics that really stuck with me:

> *And when one of us is gone*
> *And one of us is left to carry on*
> *Then remembering will have to do*

I recall thinking, What do you mean when one of us is gone?! I know my mom didn't mean to plant that concern in my head, but I was an emotionally mature child and it stuck with me, especially because the two of us were so close.

So, then, when all of my grandparents, my best friend, and my uncle died in quick succession, those memories flooded my mind, and my OCD got even worse, though I didn't know that what I was experiencing at the time were intrusive thoughts. I just knew that from then on, I had an overwhelming fear of losing loved ones. During this time, I was briefly prescribed Lexapro and struggled with anorexia, which gave me a warped sense of control when I otherwise felt powerless.

Yet I refused to let my struggles hinder me from pursuing my dreams. Even if my grandparents were gone, they were still with me in spirit and rooting for me to succeed. They would want me not only to finish school, but to excel in life as best I could.

In light of this, on my twenty-first birthday, which also happened to be the day after I graduated, I was ready to relocate to LA and make a name for myself in the entertainment industry, whether that was as an actress, a TV host, or a news reporter.

Conveniently, one of my college friends, Farrah, who was my first roommate in LA—and the first roommate I ever had—had a friend who worked at a private member's cigar lounge and restaurant. Every A-list celebrity, director, writer, and actor hung out there, and it was the hottest place to work in Beverly Hills. I felt really lucky to get the job. I figured I might meet the right people there, which would lead to being discovered. So, I moved to Hollywood, never anticipating just how drastically this decision would change my life forever.

I first laid eyes on Eddie Cibrian a few months later, when he stepped off the elevator at the cigar lounge, where he played poker on Tuesday nights. If you were to ask me when I was growing up what my exact type was, to a tee it was Eddie—tall, dark, and handsome, with dimples. The second we made eye contact, he smiled at me with those dimples, and I melted. How could I not? He's undeniably a gorgeous human. Our relationship wasn't romantic from the jump, though the writing was on the wall from day one.

Eddie was the sweetest, funniest, most charismatic gentleman I'd ever met. He always made me feel like I was the only girl in the room when I was working. Whereas most of the other patrons at the cigar lounge just wanted me to serve them their drinks and leave them to play poker, Eddie made a concerted effort to make eye contact with me.

He never wore a wedding ring, so I assumed he was single. I didn't know that he was famous, either, partly because I never thought to look him up. I had a Palm Treo (only the hottest phone of 2006), but it didn't have an internet browser on it, and I didn't even own a laptop. I would go to the internet cafe on Hollywood Boulevard and La Brea Avenue to use their Wi-Fi when I needed to check my email for auditions. I wasn't concerned with googling this hot guy who said he was an actor in LA. Do you know how many hot guys in LA were and still are actors? A lot! And I didn't recognize him, so I figured he couldn't be that famous.

I was just happy to be the girl working the poker game he played in. Sure, my hair reeked of cigars and I was breathing secondhand smoke every night, but the money was so good—it paid my rent and supported my shopping habits.

I loved my experience at the cigar bar for more than the money. I also became friends with all the employees. We were like a little sisterhood, all striving toward similar goals and dealing with the same BS every night. Just as I figured I would, I made so many connections with members as well. I got my first talent agent and was signed by a modeling agency because of that job. There was always someone who was Someone hanging around, whether it was a writer, a casting director, or an actor. I served Quentin Tarantino, Johnny Knoxville, Sylvester Stallone, and Steven Seagal, to name a few. Steven Seagal even gave me his phone number and called me! I didn't know what to say to him, because he was so much older, but my dad was a huge fan. Everyone who worked there wanted to be famous, so I was in good company. In fact, one of the girls is a very big country star now.

Eddie was probably one of the lesser-known people I rubbed elbows with. To be clear, he wasn't my boyfriend (at least not exclusively). But we did start a physical relationship at the end of 2006, which was a weekly booty call. After his Tuesday night poker games, and when my shift ended, we would go out together with our friends to get drinks, and then he would come back to my house, where we would hook up. (Many of his friends were married, also without rings, though I didn't know that.) Eddie would then go home, and I'd go back to my life for the rest of the week. In hindsight, it was pretty brazen of him to be fully out in public with a bunch of single women while his wife and child were at home.

I even remember one night when the paparazzi photographed us leaving Les Deux, a nightclub in Hollywood, and it was no big deal. It wasn't like Eddie was freaking out that he'd been caught on camera with me.

Of course, I've been asked a zillion times how I didn't realize he was married. Why would I have thought he was? It never even crossed my mind. At some point, I did look at his IMDb, as my roommate was also dating an actor, and I wanted to see what movies he'd been in. The only one I'd seen was *Say It Isn't So* starring Heather Graham, and I vaguely remembered thinking Eddie's character was hot, even though I had no idea who he was at that time. This was pre–social media, so it wasn't like he was posting pics of his family in matching pajamas in front of a Christmas tree.

The frightening thing is that I totally thought I could end up with Eddie; he looked how I'd always imagined my future husband would, and he treated me well. But I wasn't trying to settle down at the age of twenty-one, and I was keeping my options open and dating other people.

That was when I started seeing Jesse Metcalfe, the sexy gardener from *Desperate Housewives*. In college, I'd watched the movie *John Tucker Must Die*, which Jesse starred in, and I recall thinking what a dream it would be to date him—which I did, beginning in early 2007. Jesse was an awesome guy, but our relationship didn't happen right away. Soon after we first met, he went to rehab, so we started hanging out often only after he finished. The first date he took me on postrehab was the *Cloverfield* red carpet movie premiere. I then spent my twenty-second birthday at dinner with him, and I vividly remember sticking to water and Red Bull all night as a way of supporting his sobriety. After dinner, we went to a karaoke bar and ended up heading out early, since everyone was drinking alcohol, and I could tell it was a little overwhelming for him. The fact that a group of my friends decided to sing Rick Springfield's "Jessie's Girl" didn't help, either. But I was totally cool with leaving and told him that I just wanted to spend my birthday with him. He also took me shopping at Neiman Marcus and told me to get whatever I wanted as a gift. I chose a pair of Marc Jacobs sunglasses that I have to this day.

Overall, Jesse and I had a great time together. We would order in dinner with his parents at his house, and—when we were alone—he would play the guitar and serenade me with songs like "Hey There Delilah." It felt like I was living a real-life fantasy with this guy I'd watched on TV and in movies for years.

But eventually we grew apart, and when things faded out later that summer, I fell right back into regularly hanging with Eddie—at which point it became more serious than our weekly poker-night hookup. So much so that when I was moving apartments, Eddie came to help me and met most of my friends and even my mother. His best friend (whom I thought was divorced) also joined us with his son, who was a toddler at the time. We were literally intertwining our families and the people closest to us.

During this period, Eddie would take me out on his boat, and we'd cruise around Castaic Lake taking photos together. It really felt like we were building something. Did I think it was weird that I never went to his house? Honestly, no. He lived in Calabasas, supposedly. And I certainly wasn't making the trek to Calabasas in 2007, when Ubers didn't exist, and I had less than $1,000 to my name. It was so much easier and more fun to hang out in Beverly Hills or Hollywood, and my place was closer and more convenient. I didn't see a single red flag, especially since we weren't exclusive.

The first crack in Eddie's perfectly constructed façade appeared one night at the cigar lounge, when one of the members approached me. He said, "Listen, Eddie is coming in tonight. And I just want to let you know—before you do something you might regret—that I heard he's married." He must have seen that we were getting more serious and didn't want me to get in too deep.

I didn't believe it (or maybe I didn't *want* to believe it) because I was wild about Eddie. And, again, we were out together all the time in public, so I didn't feel like some secret mistress! Still, I was freaking out and had a massive pit in my stomach.

As predicted, Eddie showed up and, immediately, he could tell that my energy was off. He asked me what was going on, and I told him to check his phone. I'd sent him a message saying, "I have to ask, before we hang out tonight, does something belong on your ring finger?" I didn't want to come across as aggressive or have him think I was acting crazy, since I didn't know if it was true, and also because my inherent people-pleasing tendencies were in full force. So I decided to choose pleasant and palatable, even a little playful, over direct and confrontational. I was young, and I felt like I was falling in love with him. I didn't want to rock the boat for no reason. Writing, "Are you married?" felt too accusatory, even though I now know that it would have been completely appropriate given the circumstances.

Eddie acted like he didn't understand exactly what I was getting at, so I posed the question straightforwardly. And his answer was "No, that's insane. Why would you ask me that?" It was gaslighting in its most basic form. I trusted him, so we continued hanging out.

Fast-forward another few months. My mom called me and asked, "That guy that helped you move into your apartment, the one you're kind of seeing—he's Eddie Cibrian from *Third*

Watch, right?" I replied, "Yes, he was on that show, why?" And she answered, "Well, I'm reading the newspaper right now and it says that Eddie and his wife, Brandi Glanville, are expecting their second child soon." I was shocked. Even though part of me knew the relationship was too good to be true (and also because the guy at the cigar lounge had told me), I was still surprised to hear that it was *actually* true and in print. Now Eddie couldn't deny it.

I called him immediately, and he apologized. He said he cared about me so much, that he loved spending time with me, blah, blah, blah. He threw out all the classic clichés of cheating husbands. He also claimed that his marriage wasn't working out. I was so humiliated, hurt, and, mostly, pissed. My heart sank into my stomach, and I couldn't believe that I'd been played for so long. I got that he wasn't my boyfriend, but it was still a betrayal when I thought we might have a real future together. And how could he cheat, not only on his wife, but on his child and baby-to-be? It was unfathomable to me that someone—someone I cared about!—could actually do something so deceitful. I didn't want to hear his bullshit. I said, "I want nothing to do with you ever again."

After that conversation, I intentionally started taking a television hosting seminar with Marki Costello, who's a prominent hosting coach, on Tuesday evenings, so I wasn't even tempted to pick up a shift at the cigar lounge during his weekly outing. The last thing I wanted was to run into Eddie. I still really wanted to be a TV host or an actress, so I also took acting classes with Ivana Chubbuck and Lesly Kahn. I knew that training with those women would look good on my résumé. I was ready to reset my sights on my real goal—a job in entertainment.

But, as soon as the six-month courses were over, I got asked to pick up a shift on a Tuesday night and, naturally, Eddie was still there playing poker. He asked me if we could talk after I got off work and I said okay. At the very least, I wanted to hear him out; I thought he owed me not only a conversation but a massive apology.

I had a couple more hours until my shift ended, and my heart was in my stomach the entire time. In between passing out cocktails and dodging clouds of cigar smoke, I was pounding drinks myself. I really cared about Eddie, and as much as I was disgusted with his actions, I also missed the way he made me laugh, and how I always felt safe in his company. I'd built this fantasy in my mind of what our lives could look like together.

By the time we ended up at a little dive bar on Sunset Boulevard, I was drunk. Eddie then came back to my place, where we drank more. He apologized profusely, told me that he and Brandi were separated, and that—even though she'd just given birth to their second son—they were living in separate houses. He went a step further in saying that they were planning to split for good and that he wanted to continue seeing me.

In that moment, as an intelligent human being, did part of me think he was lying? Of course. However, I had this gorgeous, charming man standing in front of me, promising that he was choosing me. I was young, maybe even a little naïve, and hoping for the best. I was also drunk, and drunk me told myself to believe him. We then had sex, which I didn't remember until I called him to confirm the next day. I also reconfirmed that he was separated from Brandi. When he said yes, I agreed to give us another go, and we started hanging out again toward the end of 2008.

Soon after we reconciled, Eddie bought me a pair of diamond earrings as an "I'm sorry" gift for the "confusion" about his marital status. He told me he loved me, which made me think things might be heading in a serious direction. I was still only twenty-three years old, so I wasn't intent on nailing him down. I was just enjoying hanging out with him, which included a snowboarding trip that February to Mammoth Mountain with many of his friends and mine. We got a bunch of hotel rooms, and I was so excited because it would be the first time Eddie and I would spend multiple nights sleeping together, just the two of us. There had been a few occasions when he'd passed out at my apartment for a bit, but nothing more.

While we were in Mammoth, Eddie taught me how to snowboard. He was already so good, which was very attractive. Meanwhile, I had no idea what I was doing, so he went to the ski shop, rented all the equipment I needed, and started with the basics. The bunny hills in Mammoth are not for beginners, but he helped me every step of the way, even when I was frustrated.

At the end of a full day of snowboarding, I remember sitting in the hot tub with his phone right on the edge. I saw it light up with a name I recognized. I said, "LeAnn Rimes is calling you?" And he replied, "Yeah, I just did a movie with her in Canada called *Northern Lights*." I couldn't believe it. I was such a LeAnn Rimes fan growing up. She was the youngest person to win a Grammy, at age fourteen, which was iconic, and she was also in one of my favorite movies, *Coyote Ugly*. I thought it was so cool that he knew her.

Even though we were taking things slow, that trip seemed like a huge step in our relationship. Our friends had so much fun with each other, and I loved playing cohostess with him. Going to sleep in the same bed and waking up next to each other made it feel like we were heading in the right direction.

Until about a month later, in March 2009, on St. Patrick's Day, when I had plans with Eddie and his best friend to visit my friend Stacie at work (Stacie was the bartender on *The Hills*). Then we were all going to hang out after. But, before we met up, I got a call from Eddie's best friend saying Eddie wasn't going to make it. I thought, Why? What now?

When I questioned him, his best friend shared the news that the following morning Eddie's affair with LeAnn Rimes was going to be on the cover of *Us Weekly* and splashed all over the internet. Apparently, they'd been caught on surveillance cameras being affectionate with each other over dinner in Laguna Beach. Was he fucking kidding me? I was so furious. I vowed never to speak to Eddie again (for the second time).

It wasn't just that I felt betrayed, even if that was part of it. It brought me back to cheating on the boyfriend I had throughout high school and college. Even as a sixteen-year-old girl I felt gross and ashamed to disrespect someone in that way. I knew then that I'd never be unfaithful again. So when the news story came out exposing Eddie for stepping out on Brandi with LeAnn, I felt like, Oh my God, how can you be cheating on your wife with not one, but two women? Doesn't it rot your insides?

I also felt like a complete idiot for believing him. Clearly, I was seeing and hearing what I wanted to and ignoring all of the noise outside of that. I was so infatuated with him, and I wanted to be loved and validated so badly that I blocked out the fact that he was a total piece of shit. I felt like a fool for believing him and couldn't comprehend why he'd lie to me if he actually cared about me.

Above all, because I was seeing red in that moment, I wanted revenge and I wanted my voice heard. I figured that was the only way to regain the power it felt like he had taken from me. As far as I was concerned, Eddie had made me look stupid, and I was prepared to return that favor.

This was when a friend of mine tipped off a tabloid that Eddie and I were still seeing each other and that he'd been at my house one night after the LeAnn affair was public. Even though that detail wasn't true, I didn't care. I wanted him to burn. So, when the tabloid reached out, I said, "Yeah, maybe he was."

I imagine that Eddie must have had his lawyer threaten to sue the tabloid—

—because they got in touch with me again and asked me to sign legal documents saying it was true that he'd been with me post-LeAnn. Since the story had already run, and the tip had come from a friend of mine, they'd assumed it was accurate. I would have let it play out, just to screw Eddie, but once they sent me the legal document, there was no way I was going to confirm it.

The only time I spoke to Eddie after that was when he and his friend contacted me on a three-way phone call to ask if I could do Eddie a favor, meet with his lawyer, and go on the record saying he'd never cheated on LeAnn with me. If you can believe it, I actually agreed. I remember driving to Beverly Hills, walking into his lawyer's office, and signing a different legal document saying that we'd never had relations once his relationship with LeAnn had been exposed. Why did I appease him? Because I'm a fucking people pleaser! I didn't know how to say no, couldn't imagine facing the pushback if I did. And I thought, You know what, LeAnn, good luck! You're both cheaters. You deserve each other. I don't want to be a part of this anymore. He's a scumbag. Good riddance.

It did piss me off that Eddie never had the balls to have a final conversation with me, and that he had to have his friend on the call about the false story. But I got over it, and I haven't seen Eddie since.

I've been asked many times if I regret my relationship with Eddie. Honestly, it's hard to beat yourself up about dating a married man when you didn't know he was married. He lied to me repeatedly when I wanted nothing more than to trust him. What I do feel badly about is that, after I found out, I didn't think about the impact on Brandi and their kids. Or how it would damage her to learn that we'd had this relationship for two years and then to watch me being interviewed about it on television. I couldn't see beyond my own hurt and betrayal from Eddie or conceive of how it would feel to be his wife and the mother of his kids. I've come a long way since then. I'm not that young, naïve girl anymore. And I'm truly sorry for the pain that Brandi and those boys suffered. No one deserves that.

Fortunately, I found a way to distract myself from the whole Eddie situation—by going to John Mayer's house for some *fun*. I was feeling disheartened, and I really wanted some distraction from the hurt and confusion Eddie left me with. I'd first met John in October 2008, when I worked at his birthday party. He was with Jennifer Aniston at the time, but they broke up shortly thereafter.

Once we'd connected at his birthday, John came to the cigar lounge one night and had his friend ask for my phone number. When I said yes, John then asked me if I was free later that evening. I told him we could go back to my apartment, which was close by and that he could enter through the garage in the back, so he wasn't seen in front of the building. I didn't want him to think I was this girl trying to show off that I was with John Mayer. John knew that there were going to be a few friends at my place, and it wasn't a problem.

That particular night, my friend Jordan was over, as I was living with his cousin, Tara. Jordan was an aspiring musician, and I remember John coming over with his friend Melvin and borrowing his guitar so he could play us a song, while we all drank some New Castles and hung out.

After that night, John and I were casually involved for about six months. (And, yes, Eddie and John did overlap, which was fine, as I wasn't exclusive with either of them.) John and I didn't see each other every day, but we talked on the phone a fair amount—he seemed really into phone sex, which was a first for me and a little awkward, but I was willing to do whatever he wanted.

Overall, we just really enjoyed each other's company; he was so nice and respectful to me. Honestly, being with John was like another dream come true. Every time I saw him, I felt like someone should pinch me. I would think: How is John Mayer in my house? How am I in John Mayer's house? I kept it so quiet because I wanted to continue hanging out with him.

Unfortunately, since it wasn't always just the two of us, one of my girlfriends opened her big mouth, word got around the cigar lounge, and the wrong person found out. That person, who ultimately sold us out, was a girl who'd been fired from the cigar lounge for sleeping with another member. John was not a member of the LA club, but unbeknownst to me, he was a member of the New York club, and it was against the rules for an employee to have a physical relationship with a member, so I got fired. This hadn't been an issue with Eddie, since he was not a member.

Anyway, this woman went to the tabloids and told them about me and John. Once it was public, he didn't want to speak to me or see me anymore. And I understood. For all he knew, I was the one blabbing about the details of our hangouts.

At that point, I was so fed up with being used by men that I decided to do an interview about him so I could at least set the record straight on the tabloid reporting about us. It might not have been the best move, looking back, but I wasn't a public figure and couldn't afford a publicist in those days. And while I may have been a people pleaser, I wasn't going to let someone walk all over me, not even John Mayer.

There was a bright side to all of these unfortunate events. If I hadn't been fired from the cigar lounge, I never would have started working at Villa Blanca, which also means that if John and I hadn't hooked up, *Vanderpump Rules* might not exist.

5

THE BUTTERFLY EFFECT

n the summer of 2009, I moved into my own apartment for the first time. I'd had roommates during my first three years in LA, and I felt like I needed my own space after everything that had happened with Eddie and John. I found this really cute studio apartment in Hollywood, in the Fontenoy building, which looked like the Tower of Terror at Disney. It was built in the 1920s, so it even had one of those elevators where you have to close the gate once you're inside. Being one block north of Hollywood Boulevard was the coolest place to live, so the location was perfect, too. I was in walking distance to tons of bars, restaurants, and clubs. When I went out at night, I'd bring a bigger purse that fit a pair of flip-flops so I could walk home and carry my high heels.

As soon as I was settled, I got a cat and named her Penny

Lane. As happy as I was to live alone, it didn't hurt to have a little company. She's been through everything with me, so I promised her that my current house would be her final residence. If there's one thing cats hate, it's moving!

The best part of living at the Fontenoy, and with Penny alone, was having independence, and the ability to do what I wanted when I wanted, without anyone else's input. I would walk to the bars on Hollywood Boulevard all the time with my friends who worked at the cigar lounge and other neighborhood restaurants. There was one cute little establishment in particular called Essex (now Jameson's) that we frequented, in part because I liked the bar manager. His name was Collin. We had mutual friends, so I kind of knew him by association, and I'd heard he was a good guy. Not only that, but he was just a normal person, as in *not* a celebrity. He wasn't trying to be famous or land acting gigs like everyone else in LA, and I appreciated that about him. In a way, he reminded me of the guys from back home in Azusa. He had a regular job but was still cool and in the scene, with a natural swagger.

I said to myself, okay, Scheana, you've tried dating (or at least hanging out and hooking up with) all of these celebrities—Jesse Metcalfe, Eddie Cibrian, John Mayer, Shemar Moore, Josh Hopkins, Shane West, Jesse McCartney, JC Chasez, Adrian Grenier, Ricardo Chavira, William Tell, two actors from *The Notebook*, and a few NFL, NBA, and MLB players, to name a few—and that's not really working out. It's time to switch things up and date someone who's under the radar. I didn't want any of the fanfare or complications that came with being linked to someone famous. I wanted to be with someone who was grounded.

So Collin and I started hanging out often, sometimes at his

place, sometimes at mine. The "his place" part was key, because I definitely wasn't about to hook up with another married man. I'll never forget one specific night when we watched the movie *I Love You, Man*, and there was this scene where the two leads go to a Rush concert. I was a big classic rock fan growing up, and my parents listened to Rush, so seeing that band in the movie made me wish I could go to a Rush concert, too. The scene stuck with me, and to this day, whenever I hear one of their songs, I think of Collin.

He was such a solid guy. I remember that for Easter in 2010, when my sister, Cortney, was around twelve years old, he went and got us all the ingredients to make ice cream sundaes for her. She thought it was supercool to come spend time with me and my friends in Hollywood and sleep over at my place on an occasional weekend. It gave her a little taste of my world, even though she was much younger, and Collin's thoughtfulness made this visit even more memorable for her.

I wouldn't say that Collin and I were boyfriend and girlfriend, though I wasn't really talking to anyone else for the six months we were hooking up. I didn't think he was, either. Then one night, when I was at the bar with one of my girlfriends, this pretty brunette girl, who would visit him all the time, came in. My friend and I were sitting there chatting and having a drink, when I saw Collin outside kissing this woman. I was gutted. It felt like my experience with Eddie all over again. I understood that we weren't exclusive, but it was still so disrespectful of Collin to do that when he knew full well that I was there. In that moment, I realized that he was clearly hanging out with both of us. Not cool at all.

I was so upset that my friend and I were like, Screw him,

we're leaving. Of course, Collin spotted us heading out and noticed how pissed I was, so my friend went back to my place to give us a chance to talk. Collin started walking with me, and immediately began saying, "I'm just not good enough for you. Look at the guys you've been dating. They're celebrities. That's not me, and I could never be that." Basically, he was self-sabotaging. I told him that being with famous people wasn't what I wanted, that I wanted a normal, family-oriented, good guy, whom I could feel safe with and who wasn't going to cheat on me. "You just kissed that girl right in front of my face. That is the opposite of what I want." And he repeated his fear that he would never be enough for me. It went on like that for the entire walk back to my place, but my mind had already been made up. After what I went through with Eddie, I had no room for liars or cheaters in my life.

Finally, Collin left me alone, and I should have moved on peacefully. But in true twenty-five-year-old Scheana fashion, I thought, You know what, you screwed me over so now I'm going to screw your best friend. Makes total sense, right?

Collin's best friend, whom I already knew, was living and working in Las Vegas at the time. Naturally, I decided to take a girls' trip to Vegas—where I'd been road-tripping to clubs and concerts since I was eighteen—with the full intent of hooking up with him as a means of hurting Collin. And if you think I didn't follow through with it, you'd be wrong. Oh, sweet revenge. I couldn't wait for it to get back to Collin.

While I was in Vegas, I updated my Facebook status to say that I was there. Vintage 2010 move. Soon, Michael Shay from high school commented that he was there with all of the guy friends I grew up with and played baseball with. Crazy how the Butterfly

Effect works. Had Collin not kissed that girl at the bar, I wouldn't have gone to Vegas that weekend to get back at him by banging his friend, and I never would have reconnected with Shay.

After we left Vegas, Shay and I kept in touch. It just so happened that I was moving a few weeks later, so he and all those same guys helped me move into my new apartment at Park La Brea—where I lived for eight years. After that, Shay and I started dating.

Even though it didn't work out with Collin, I was still looking for a "normal" guy, and Shay was exactly that. I hadn't been in a serious relationship for almost five years, and I was ready to settle down with a nice person. It just seemed like the right thing to do, and Shay felt like home to me.

About a year into us dating, Shay and I ran into Collin at this sports bar on Melrose called the Parlor, which sadly didn't survive the pandemic. At this point Shay and I were still in the honeymoon stage of our relationship. I felt so lucky to have reconnected with this person who'd become my best friend, not just the cute sophomore I'd carpooled with in high school. I introduced Collin to Shay, and he bought us shots of Jameson. That was our thing, either Jameson with beer or with a diet Coke. I was such a whiskey girl.

A few days later, Collin texted me and said it was really good to see me, that things with the girl at the bar didn't work out, and that he regretted what had happened between us. Seeing me with Shay, he realized I actually did want someone who wasn't famous, and that he should have stayed with me. I also think that girl ended up cheating on him. Karma. He said that his life would have been so much better if he'd picked me, and that he was very depressed.

I didn't understand the magnitude of what he was telling me. When you're twenty-six, you don't always get how much you can make a difference in someone's life. Or how heavy the world can be for some people. I had been depressed when I was younger, but I'd never thought about doing anything drastic. So I was kind of like, Well, that's what you get for making the wrong decision. I was right there. You kissed a girl in front of my face. You hurt me.

It was the last conversation I ever had with him. I couldn't imagine there would be more serious consequences, but one week after that, Collin killed himself.

I'll never forget the moment I found out. I was working at Villa Blanca, and my friend Matt texted me: *Did you hear about Collin?* I replied: *I talked to him last week, what's up?* He then told me that Collin had driven to the top of Mulholland Drive and taken his own life. I read the words on my phone again, but I couldn't believe what Matt was telling me was real. I was completely hysterical. It felt as if I was floating outside of my own body. I could barely breathe.

I clearly was in no condition to finish my shift, so I got off early and Tina McDowell drove me around the corner to Shay, who was bartending close by. I remember sitting in the car with her and just crying my eyes out. Not only was Collin gone, but I'd been so inconsiderate during our last interaction. I replayed it a million times in my head. I asked myself over and over, If I'd been kinder, would he have still killed himself? I knew I wasn't to blame and that he'd been dealing with a million other things, but the guilt was still there, weighing heavily on my chest.

There was one night after Collin passed away that I had the most vivid dream I've ever had in my life. I was at a house I didn't recognize and there was a knock on the door. When I opened it, Collin was standing there. He said, "I'm so sorry. I didn't mean to do it. I changed my mind at the last minute, and it was too late." Then he gave me the biggest hug. I actually felt this hug in my sleep. So much so that when I woke up, his presence was with me. I was physically shaken and couldn't escape the dream all day.

For years after his passing, whenever I would go to an audition in the Valley, I would avoid Mulholland Drive. It took me totally out of my way, but I just couldn't get myself to drive through an area that felt so haunted by sad memories. Finally, there was one time when I was running so late that I had no choice but to take Mulholland. So, I mentally prepared myself. Right as I got to the road's peak, the Rush song from *I Love You, Man* came on the radio.

In that moment, I knew, without a doubt, that Collin's spirit was there. From then on, I felt comfortable taking Mulholland, which I now do almost every day when I drive my daughter to school. I felt like, with that sign, maybe he was telling me that he was okay and that he shared the same fond memories of our relationship. I still think about him every single time.

Years passed, but I kept the long-expired Hershey's chocolate bottle from the day we made ice cream sundaes in my refrigerator. Gross as that may sound, I just couldn't get rid of it. It was the only thing I had left of him because back then, camera phones weren't really a thing. I might have a couple of photos of us on a very old laptop or on my MySpace page, but that's about it. When I moved into a new apartment after Fontenoy, I even brought the Hershey's bottle with me, and my mom threw it out one day when she was cleaning my refrigerator. I was devastated. Deep down, I knew I couldn't keep it forever, but I also wasn't ready to let it go, even though things with Collin didn't exactly end well.

For years I was so angry at him, because I used to see suicide as such a selfish act. I thought you only hurt the people around you. It wasn't until a couple of years ago, when I lost a friend from high school, that I started looking at it from the suicidal person's perspective. A mutual friend said to me, "Scheana, think about the mindset she must have been in; she was in such a dark place that she wasn't thinking about her kids or her family." That definitely changed my view. I finally understood how scary and difficult it must have been in her and Collin's heads to push them that far.

Collin was deeply troubled in the end, and maybe there was nothing anyone could have done to save him. There were so many people who loved him, and hundreds of them were at his celebration of life. He was just twenty-eight when we lost him. He had a full future ahead of him, and, for whatever reason, he wanted a way out.

I have such a different outlook on suicide after losing two friends, and I will always take anyone who is having suicidal thoughts and feelings seriously. It's so important to be there for your loved ones, because you never know what another person is going through. Being able to forgive and move forward with someone in your life, even if they've hurt you, is a gift that should not be taken for granted.

I forgive Collin. And, every year, on his birthday and the day he passed, I do a shot of Jameson for him.

May you rest in peace.

6

ALMOST FAMOUS

When Collin passed away, I was already working at Villa Blanca. As soon as I was fired from my job at the cigar lounge, I had called my friend from college, who'd recently started bartending there. It was the week of my birthday, and I had rent to pay and a celebration to fund. Thankfully, the owner of the cigar lounge had given me a month's severance and also said he'd provide me with a stellar reference. He understood that I was a diligent employee and that he'd had no choice but to let me go for a rule I'd unknowingly broken, even though he didn't want to. So, I didn't panic immediately. Villa Blanca was close by, and I loved working in Beverly Hills—everything from the clientele to the money to the area, which felt like home. I also wanted to stay in the vicinity because I still wanted to be an actress. My world revolved around auditions and trying to make it in the business. Villa Blanca was centrally located, and I thought I had a good shot at landing a new job there.

On a good day I'd have multiple auditions, which sometimes meant driving from the west side back to Hollywood in rush hour traffic, praying I'd make my last one on time. Often, I'd change in my car in between, depending on the parts I was going for. As scary and stressful as it could be, it was comforting to have a number of friends in the same industry going through the same ups and downs. Theatrical auditions were the most intense, whereas commercials and music videos were easy and fun, since they didn't require memorizing lines. I booked a role on *Jonas* on the Disney Channel in 2009, and later *90210* in 2010, and *Victorious* in 2011, plus some other small projects. Booking roles, especially on shows I already watched, was an adrenaline rush and the best kind of validation for me. It made me feel like all of the acting classes I'd taken were paying off and that I was on the right path.

When I got the audition to be the Pizza Girl on *Jonas*, I was so excited. Even if it wasn't my big break, I thought it would at least be a cool story for my then middle-school-aged sister to tell her friends. When the day came, there were about thirty other girls at the audition, all of whom were most certainly Pizza Girl teenage-boy-fantasy caliber. I was shocked when I got the callback. Callbacks were so nerve-wracking because you were up against the best of the best and the stakes were much higher.

Auditioning for roles was much different from, say, trying out for the cheerleading squad or the baseball team when I was in school. Growing up, I made all of the teams. As an auditioning adult, I had to face the most rejection I'd ever experienced in my entire life, which was demoralizing at times, but it also helped me build a thicker skin and I knew it was part of the business.

Ultimately, I landed the part of Pizza Girl, and when I met Nick, Joe, and Kevin Jonas during the shoot, they couldn't have been nicer. It was crazy to think that whole stadiums were screaming and losing their minds for the three down-to-earth guys on set with me. They were perfect gentlemen, purity rings and all. We shot on a closed set, and honestly, it was a lot of fun, though also high pressure and nerve-wracking, since the Jonas Brothers were so popular and the episode revolved around my character.

As I said earlier, I always wanted to be a Disney kid growing up, and although I was twenty-three when it happened, it still felt like I was living that dream. The fact that I not only got to act with the Jonas Brothers, but also had a song written about me and starred in their music video, was mind-blowing. I will forever be "Maria the Pizza Girl" to adoring Disney fans around the world.

I'll never forget how Nick Jonas was so nervous when he had to pull me by the hand in one scene. To be fair, he was a sixteen-year-old kid telling a twenty-three-year-old woman that he just wrote a song about her, so I cut him some slack. He was a total professional, but it was endearing.

Later, when I did the guest role on *Victorious*, I remember one of the supporting actresses walking around the set singing to herself and thinking, Oh my God, she has the most beautiful voice I've ever heard. What is she doing on this show and not in a recording studio? And how is she not *the* star of this show? That girl was Ariana Grande. What can I say? I have amazing taste.

In addition to scripted TV, I also dipped my toe in the reality TV pond with *The Hills* in 2009. To set the scene, it was season five, episode three of the show, and I was at a club called H.Wood in Hollywood with my friends Stacie and Brooke. We knew which cast members were going to be there, but we were told to act surprised when we saw them. At first, we spotted Spencer Pratt and his friends sitting on a couch. Heidi Montag and Stephanie Pratt were scheduled to arrive imminently. What we did not know was that we'd be called "whores" and "sluts," and that Stacie would be dubbed a "homewrecker." That word seemed to be thrown around a lot back then!

At the time, I really thought I had a handle on how these shows worked. I couldn't have been more wrong. *The Hills* wasn't real. All of the cattiness and bad blood disappeared when we weren't filming. There was one time I took my mic off after shooting a scene, and Heidi Montag pulled up in her car next to me. She was so sweet, nothing like the mean girl MTV Heidi who was edited and packaged for the masses. She said, "Hey guys, sorry I had to be mean to you, it was all just for the show. You know that, right?"

Of course it didn't much matter to me, as I wasn't planning to be a reality TV star! My goal was to concentrate on other acting gigs and getting another day job to pay the bills in the meantime, which I hoped would be with the same clientele I'd served at the cigar lounge. So when my friend from college said I should stop by and meet the owners of Villa Blanca, who were in house, I was game. They'd just opened their doors the previous day, so my friend knew they were looking for more staff.

After picking up my final check from the cigar lounge, I walked straight over to Villa Blanca, and Ken Todd—Lisa

Vanderpump's husband—was there. I informed him that I was looking for a position ASAP, and, pretty immediately, he told me that I wasn't very cute and didn't have much personality. At first, I was confused, but then realized it was his dry British sense of humor. Ha ha. He followed it up with, "Can you start today?" I replied, "Is tomorrow an option?" And, thankfully, Ken said yes.

The next day, I returned to Villa Blanca for the lunch shift. My first impression of the restaurant was that it was absolutely beautiful. The décor was all white and silver with the largest, most stunning fresh floral arrangements. The employees—who looked like they'd just stepped out of a magazine—wore uniforms that were cute enough to transition from work to social plans, and the food was beyond delicious. I felt like I'd really lucked out.

While I was being trained, I met Ken and Lisa's daughter, Pandora, and all of the other employees, who were very nice and welcoming. At the end of my shift, Pandora asked me if I could stay and work a double for dinner. I took that as a good sign of things to come.

Of course, that night, at table 101, I had to serve Ken, Lisa, and four of their friends, which was intimidating right out of the gate. I didn't even know the menu yet, which meant that I totally screwed up their order. Ken asked for the ahi tuna, and I thought he meant the Crudo Ahi Tuna appetizer. When I placed it in front of him, he said, "What the fuck is this?" Politely, I replied, "It's the ahi tuna. That's what you ordered." Immediately and sternly, he corrected me. "I wanted the seared ahi tuna entree. If you were unsure, you should have checked with me."

In that moment, I was certain I was going to be fired, on day one no less. My stomach dropped. But I pulled myself together, corrected my mistake, and they let me keep my job. *That* was my first real introduction to Ken and Lisa and how particular and meticulous they were about every single detail. In the weeks to come, I learned that Ken sometimes likes his beer in a wineglass. Meanwhile, Lisa prefers only half a glass of rosé, which is funny because she'll have multiple half glasses. And, if Lisa decides to choose tea instead, she has to have milk with it. If you serve her tea without a side of milk, you may as well go home. They're also very specific when it comes to the lighting, the flowers, and the banquet pillows with a hand chop down the middle. If those elements aren't spot-on, you get in trouble. To this day, a chopped pillow sends a shiver down my spine.

I'll never forget one night when I showed up with a 102 fever, at Pandora's insistence, and was reprimanded for giving Tyler Perry rock shrimp instead of prawns in his pasta, which wasn't even on the menu. Crustacean confusion aside, I don't know how I even made it through my shift or how I drove to work. I could barely think straight, much less serve at the top of my game. Nowadays—post-COVID—if you have the smallest sniffle you're shunned and sent home! Though I will give a shout-out to Tyler Perry as one of the best tippers ever. Typically he'd leave $200. That night was the lowest he'd ever given me, but it was still 40 percent of the bill, which was so generous, given that I'd screwed up his very simple order.

Still, mishaps notwithstanding, I loved working at Villa Blanca, which I did for about five years, first while I was single and then after I married Shay. My fellow employees got to see both sides of me—single, crazy Hollywood Scheana and serious-relationship Scheana—so it felt like my colleagues really got me. And, despite the fact that everyone knew about the Eddie affair, since photos were published in a magazine and then passed around by the staff and in the Villa Blanca kitchen, no one held it against me. The environment among the staff was just super chill and respectful.

After I'd been working at Villa Blanca for a little over a year, Lisa got cast on *The Real Housewives of Beverly Hills*. She was the Queen of Beverly Hills—gorgeous, with the poshest accent, and someone I always strived to impress—so she felt like British royalty, moonlighting as my boss in LA. All to say I wasn't very surprised when she was tapped for the latest *Housewives* franchise.

Lisa was already very demanding, and the whole staff was terrified that she was going to become a diva once she was on TV. You did not want to upset her. Honestly, I would have rather disappointed my parents than Lisa—she's a perfectionist like I am, and she expected everyone to be at the top of their game. She was also someone I looked up to, not only as a business owner but as a mother. She had both of her kids working hard for her, even though she had enough money that they probably never needed to work a day in their lives. I really respected that.

To the whole staff's pleasant surprise, once Lisa got the show, we actually saw a softer side of her. She had more interest in getting to know her staff, and she seemed to ease up on the aesthetic demands at Villa Blanca, unless they were filming, since she now had so many other concerns. I have to say, I was a little relieved.

From there, I began taking on double shifts, sometimes serving and sometimes bartending, which I learned while I was there. The money was good and I had become someone Ken and Lisa knew they could count on. That was how Tom Sandoval and I became friends—we would bartend together on the weekends.

Tom and I had similar interests, were close in age, and got along from the get-go. Our love for classic rock music was one of the first things we bonded over. During our shifts, we talked about auditioning and our mutual dreams of being on *Dancing with the Stars* one day. (Ironic, I know.) We worked well together—with one of us making drinks for the tables and the other tending to the patrons sitting at the bar. As time went on, we grew closer as friends because we clicked and really understood each other. It felt nice to have someone I knew I could rely on in a setting that could be so stressful.

As much as I loved serving, being behind the bar was even more fun. On slower days, I got to chat with customers like Dustin Hoffman and other celebrities I admired. I also rubbed elbows with La Toya Jackson, Priscilla Presley, Sharon Stone, Stevie Wonder, and Ray Liotta, to name a few, which all felt very glamorous and like I was getting closer to my dream.

I worked as many holidays as I could, because we got to put auto gratuity on every table. It would be a set menu and a set price, so it was guaranteed money. On Valentine's Day and New Year's Eve at Villa Blanca, I'd walk away with thousands of dollars. One time I pocketed $1,400 in a single shift, which was my rent for the month. It was insane. Not to mention that we had so much fun, and I made so many good friends—many of whom I still hang out with.

Villa Blanca was the opposite of catty. Everyone who worked there had the same passions, and we were very supportive of each other. Just like at the cigar lounge, it felt like a family. We helped each other with side work instead of demanding that the new employees do it all. Even though we didn't pull tips, we knew we could count on one another when we got in the weeds. When it wasn't as busy as usual, we'd spend time venting about bad auditions and personal drama. On the more crowded nights, it was go, go, go, and then we'd head out for drinks together. Sometimes we even stayed after hours at Villa Blanca, where Pandora's husband, Jason Sabo, would DJ. It was a big dance party. One time, I even sparked up a bowl with Ariana behind the bar. Sorry, Lisa!

It wasn't until July 2011, when I was asked to work a party at SUR—another of Lisa and Ken's restaurants, which was in West Hollywood—that things changed drastically for me. While Villa Blanca was a peaceful playground, SUR was a lion's den.

Regardless, I was so honored that Lisa asked me, along with Tom Sandoval and Tina McDowell, to moonlight at SUR for the night. They already had a full staff, but they were opening up a brand-new lounge and garden section, so they needed extra hands on deck. SUR was the cool, sexier sister restaurant of Villa Blanca and definitely a place I wanted to work. For one, they had photoshoots on par with something out of *Maxim* magazine. And I'd seen paparazzi photos of Britney Spears leaving through the back door of SUR into the infamous alley, which was iconic.

There was also a part of me that was nervous, because I wasn't sure if I'd end up on *The Real Housewives of Beverly Hills*. The show had filmed at Villa Blanca in the past, and I assumed it would also be filming at SUR. I'd always avoided the cameras, so as not to become a background server on a reality series that had nothing to do with me. With that said, I had zero suspicion that I was walking into a setup for a spin-off when I agreed to work the launch party, nor that it would ultimately position me as a fool on national television.

That night, when the guests started arriving, I spotted Brandi Glanville immediately and was *terrified*. I remember pulling Tina over and saying, "Oh my God! Do you see that tall blonde woman right there? She's the ex-wife of that actor guy I was dating a few years ago." Tina remarked, "Holy shit. Go over there and make good TV." I shook my head. "No fucking way. I need to go home."

As Tina and I were chatting about what I should do, Lisa came over and said, "Get your asses to work. What are you doing talking? Scheana, go over to those women over there and tray-pass hors d'oeuvres." She pointed to where Brandi was standing with her friends. I was completely panicked, but how could I say no to Lisa?

I took a long, deep breath, and holding a tray of goat cheese balls, I walked over to Brandi's vicinity, trying to keep my face hidden by looking down at the ground while balancing the balls. Obviously, I wasn't inconspicuous enough, as I heard Brandi say, "Oh, there's that She-Anna Marie girl." I was freaking out, assuming she was going to make a massive scene. I looked at her awkwardly and smiled before hurrying over to Lisa to explain the situation.

Naturally, Lisa acted as though she was shocked and instructed me to go home. She said she had no idea that I used to sleep with Brandi's husband, though some would say that's hard to believe, since everyone at Villa Blanca, including Lisa's daughter, Pandora, knew. I think Lisa just wanted to keep her hands clean while catching both me and Brandi off guard.

Either way, I went straight home, fearful that Shay was going to break up with me when I was portrayed as a home-wrecking whore on national television, a title that the clique of girls at SUR would later brand me with. Thankfully, Shay was very understanding and recognized that it was something from my past and not my fault.

Unfortunately, not everyone shared Shay's opinion. That same night, before I'd been sent home, I'd tried to talk to Stassi Schroeder—who was on staff at SUR—about it. At first, I really liked Stassi and thought we were going to become fast friends. I told her that I was super stressed out and she asked what was wrong, in what seemed to be a compassionate way. Turns out, not so much! As soon as I shared the details about the Eddie-Brandi situation, she was instantly disgusted. In a snotty, judgmental tone, she asked, "What do you mean you were sleeping with her husband?" I said, "I didn't know he was married." She didn't buy it and quickly turned on me. She also got some of the other women at SUR to give me the mean-girl treatment, and I felt like I was back in middle school, being bullied all over again.

Shortly after we'd filmed the finale for *RHOBH*, rumors began circulating about a potential spin-off show. And to sell a show you needed more than just a group of friends. There had to be conflict. With conflict came drama. With drama came ratings.

By October, the staff at SUR, along with a few of us from Villa Blanca, were filming the pilot for *Vanderpump Rules*. That original cast was me, Stassi, Jax Taylor, Katie Maloney, Tom Sandoval, and Kristen Doute. Tina and Peter Madrigal became "friends" of the primaries.

Shooting the pilot was exciting and scary all at once. Knowing that there was controversy surrounding me because of my past, and that it was something I was going to have to face with an audience, was daunting. At the same time, I was hoping the show would be a success, like *The Hills*. Never, in my wildest dreams, did I think we'd have almost twice as many seasons.

Shortly after we filmed the pilot, I made sure that my Botox was fresh. I didn't want to be accused of "getting work done" when the show aired. Now, as a seasoned reality TV star, I know that the irony of learning how to do your makeup better and figuring out your "good side" on camera is that people will still say you've had plastic surgery, which I have not. Trust me, if I had, I'd be shouting out my surgeon for a deal!

A few months later, *Vanderpump Rules* was greenlit, and we started officially filming season one in the summer of 2012. It first aired January 7, 2013.

Almost from the start of my employment, I was Lisa's favorite because I did whatever she asked of me. If she said jump, I asked how high. Again, this was the people pleaser in me, which didn't thrill some of my female coworkers once we started the show. There was one time at Villa Blanca when Lisa even asked me to walk over to Rite Aid to buy her mother a birthday card. She hated the first card I got and had me go back to the store and try again while someone else watched my tables. Even though I couldn't always satisfy her particular standards, she never had an assistant, so that position kind of became an extension of my job as a server.

Initially, I was a little worried about taking a full-time gig on reality TV. I had been on track to do scripted, and that was really my dream. I was concerned that if I became known for being a reality star, I'd be pigeonholed, and that it could potentially jeopardize my acting career.

But, because of my prior experience on *The Hills*, I thought *Vanderpump Rules* would be the same, especially since it had one of the same producers. If I had a scene where I sparred with Stassi, Kristen, or Katie, once cameras were down, surely we'd be able to bounce back into a friendly rapport as I'd witnessed with Heidi years earlier, right? (Wrong.) I also figured it might help me get more hosting gigs, which I was still very much interested in.

For the first several seasons, I'd often receive early morning phone calls from my restaurant boss and executive producer, Lisa Vanderpump. I felt like she was tutoring me, and I wanted to get an A in *Vanderpump Rules*.

While I can't recall exact details of phone calls from a decade ago, I remember I'd be in bed with Shay, and the phone would ring. It would be like 7 a.m. And he would say, "Oh, is it Lisa again?" And she'd be giving me suggestions on things that she wanted to have conveyed in the narrative without directly influencing it herself. I don't know if other cast members were getting these same calls, but I didn't let on. I questioned if I was being manipulated or if this was normal. Regardless, I went along with it because I wanted to make Lisa happy...and keep my job.

These calls declined during season seven. James Kennedy made a comment body-shaming Katie Maloney at SUR's party during West Hollywood's Pride Festival, resulting in Katie telling Lisa during a staff meeting that she wanted James fired from the restaurant or she would quit. Lisa was hoping that I would speak up for James and defend him, as she didn't want to let him go. As the meeting unfolded and my mouth stayed shut,

I got the death stare from Lisa. I didn't want to defend James's behavior, but I felt the pressure to say something. I chimed in to suggest that Katie not work on Tuesdays when James was doing his weekly DJ set, but that wasn't enough. Our relationship took a turn after that.

Other times, these calls weren't necessarily related to *VPR* but Lisa's personal brand. When one of her fellow housewives had made a comment that Lisa reeked of cigarettes, she opined that nobody had her back. "I can't tell you what to tweet, but here's a suggestion of what might be good for you to post..." She had a roundabout way of getting me, and others, to do her bidding, without giving a clear directive, and she would be disappointed if we didn't do what she wanted. And I never wanted to let her down.

When I first sat down with one of the executive producers to share my hesitation about diving into a reality TV show headfirst, he told me that their goal was to feature people in the service industry who were trying to make it in the entertainment world and that they'd follow me on auditions and whatever else I was passionate about. That sounded appealing to me.

It would take years for me to realize this wasn't the case.

The irony was that while we were filming the first two seasons, I was still working at Villa Blanca and SUR, making more money in the restaurants than I did on the show. I would often serve a lunch shift at Villa Blanca and then a dinner shift at SUR, just to pay my bills.

When I started working at SUR full time, the mean-girls treatment continued. It was like I was in the real-life version of the movie. I was the home-wrecking whore, as labeled by Stassi, Katie, and Kristen, which was one of the things that had sold the show and put me front and center in the story line. That was another reason why they hated me. There was literally nothing I could say or do to get Stassi to like me. She viewed me as a horrible person, and there was no changing her mind. Katie and Kristen typically followed whatever Stassi did, which singled me out.

This made my life at work much harder. Whoever was the lead server of each shift would delegate the side work, so when I finished, I'd have to check in with Stassi, who would make me polish all the glasses, roll the silverware, clean the coffee machines, and perform any of the other boring tasks she didn't feel like doing. Honestly, I didn't mind the grunt work, as I was new to SUR, and they'd already paid their dues. I understood that from having worked at Villa Blanca for a few years.

What I did mind was the way they treated me personally and how they gossiped about me behind my back. After having had a sort of work family at Villa Blanca, I felt so alone at SUR. Having my coworkers hate me for what felt like no reason was very isolating. I missed the days when I could shoot the shit with my fellow servers in between tasks, or feeling like I had a friendly face to rely on when a rude table set my day off course.

Truthfully, if Tom Sandoval hadn't been at SUR with me, I don't know how I would have survived. He always supported me and told the other girls that everyone had made mistakes in their past and that those mistakes didn't define who we were in the present. I certainly wasn't the only woman in the group who'd been lied to by a man (ahem, Stassi).

The night I performed at the Roxy in West Hollywood—as the opening act for Tina McDowell, singing my debut single "What I Like"—I saw my first glimmer of hope. Kristen and

Katie were backstage cheering me on. I thought, wow, it was only a few weeks ago that they were calling me a home-wrecking whore and now they want to be my friends. This is great! Then Stassi showed up for the sole purpose of making fun of me.

After the show, I saw her crying outside, because some of her friends weren't speaking to her, so I gave her a hug. She said, "Wait, we usually hate each other." I told her it didn't matter, that I would still be there for her. I knew what it was like to feel like the odd girl out, and I wouldn't wish that on anybody. Surprisingly, she accepted my gesture, and we were friends for a little while, until we fell out again.

Amazingly, I never thought about quitting *Vanderpump Rules* or leaving the restaurants during that first season. I knew that was what those women wanted. I actually didn't find out until last year, when Kristen revealed on her podcast that they had a secret meeting where they brainstormed how to get me kicked off of "their" show. However, their plan to ice me out by refusing to film with me brought the drama and conflict the audience wanted. Thanks for the job security, ladies!

Still, I knew I needed an ally, so I begged Ariana Madix—who was one of my best friends and coworkers at Villa Blanca—to join the show in season two. The producers also wanted her to film, as they knew of her close friendship with Tom Sandoval. We all figured that Kristen would sleep with one eye open if Ariana was around. It was a bit of an uphill battle, since at first Ariana wanted nothing to do with the show. Like me, she wanted to be a famous actress and worried reality TV would hurt her chances. But I promised her we'd have fun together and that it would pay off professionally as well. (I guess I was right about that.)

During those years, Tom, Ariana, and I would hang out at my apartment all the time and play the *Just Dance* game on Wii. Having friends I enjoyed spending time with on and off the clock made work not always feel like work. We were a group of people who had the best time together no matter where we were. This solid support system definitely got me through those early days working at SUR when the mean-girl treatment didn't let up.

To me, it was clear that Tom and Ariana made sense together, whereas Tom and Kristen did not. Not only did Kristen sleep with Jax but she'd also slept with one of Tom's band members and James. Tom had cheated on her, too. It was such a toxic relationship. And whenever Tom and Ariana were around each other, their faces would light up. They had kissed once at the Golden Nugget in Las Vegas, before Ariana joined the show, but they kept it a secret for a while. Kristen was always very insecure about Ariana; she could tell that Tom had a soft spot and an obvious attraction to her. There was no denying it.

There were plenty of times where Kristen would show up at Villa Blanca when I was bartending with Tom or Ariana. She'd sit at the end of the bar, drink wine, and just watch us interact with each other, because she thought one of us was trying to hook up with Tom. At the time, honestly, it felt pretty desperate. But I guess she had a woman's intuition. In the end, she was correct.

7

THE VOW

For the first two seasons of *Vanderpump Rules*, I was dating and then became engaged to Shay. While I didn't realize it at the time, I was kind of going through the motions of life, as I thought I was supposed to, not only as a young woman who wanted to become a wife, but also as a reality star who needed to keep the show interesting by sharing my big milestones on camera. And I definitely got caught up in the fairy tale.

So, when Shay and I got married in 2014 during season three, I thought I could live out that fairy tale by getting hitched on television. It all seemed so right. Shay was my best friend. I loved that we grew up in the same area, went to the same high school, were both raised Catholic, and were extremely family oriented. One thing I remember thinking when we started dating was that I never got sick of him. I always wanted him around. He was sweet and talented and had so much potential. I truly thought the show could be a place where his music career could flourish. Don't get me wrong, we had a few spats. We both had a strong love for football, although he was a Raiders fan and I was a Chargers fan, so we were rivals in that area! But little details like that didn't really matter, since we shared similar dreams, already had the same friend group, and got along so well. We rarely disagreed, and I felt like we'd be aligned in our parenting styles when we eventually had kids, especially because he was so amazing with his five nephews.

But our relationship was also about fitting into a specific plan for how I thought my life should be. We weren't kids anymore. I was twenty-nine and feeling the pressure to settle down. I'd dated/hooked up with a bunch of celebrities and experienced a very full single life, which ultimately didn't satisfy me. I loved that Shay was a seemingly normal guy who, I believed, would never cheat on me or betray me, as others had in the past. Since I really wanted a life with Shay, I put up blinders to the red flags that, in retrospect, were glaring. I just enjoyed his company so much that I looked the other way for too long.

We did do marriage counseling as a prerequisite before our wedding. There were some questions and concerns on my mind—one of which was that I thought he drank too much, even though I definitely didn't believe he was an alcoholic. But—typical Scheana—I kept my concerns to myself. Truth be told, I was nervous that if I voiced my apprehensions, Shay might leave me. I figured we'd work everything out once we'd tied the knot, and I tried to maintain a positive attitude.

Unfortunately, where there's a will, there's not always a way. The day before the wedding, I was at Voda Spa in West

Hollywood getting massages with two of my bridesmaids, Stacie and Ariana, and Katie, whom I had gotten really close with that summer leading up to the wedding. If I had been able to order another dress in time, Katie would have been in the bridal party as well.

I confided in them that I had this unshakable feeling of cold feet, but I refused to let it rattle me. I told myself that maybe it was the awkward massage I'd just had that rubbed me the wrong way, pun intended, or maybe I was just nervous because I was getting married on national television. Regardless, I powered through, putting on a smile and trying to honor the prewedding ritual.

On July 27, Shay and I got married at Hummingbird Nest Ranch in the Santa Susana Mountains. My bridal party was my sister Cortney, Ariana, Stacie, my friends Brooke and Adri from high school, my friend Andrea from college, Jenna Willis, and Pandora. Tom Sandoval was on Shay's side. The day of the wedding, everything went wrong. That probably should have been my first warning that our union was not destined to last. At the start of the ceremony, our vocalist—who was my friend Tina McDowell—began singing before I was even in place to walk down the aisle, and I certainly wasn't going to run to the altar, not with my OCD. Everything had been choreographed exactly how I wanted it. There was a verse in the song that said, "take my hand," which was supposed to be timed to when my dad gave me away to Shay, and he, literally, took my hand. I felt like this crazy bridezilla because I was freaking out about it. My mom kept saying, "Scheana, it's fine, calm down." Yet I felt anything but calm. Again, I chalked these nerves up to standard wedding jitters.

The rest of the ceremony went smoothly, but the DJ played

the wrong entry music when they announced my bridal party at the reception, which ruined a dance we had coordinated. It was so frustrating that such a simple mistake could throw off something we had worked so hard to plan. In hindsight, I can't help but wonder if I'd have been as upset if I knew I was marrying the right person.

As a rational human being, I do understand that these were just small mishaps that probably happen at every wedding. With that said, they felt catastrophic to me. I was just so overwhelmed that even the little things started to feel huge. I couldn't admit it fully at the time, but I knew something was off, and I felt helpless—like I was making a big mistake, and it was too late to stop it. Whether that mistake was the marriage itself, or letting the wedding be filmed, I wasn't so sure. I also felt the pressure of how much money had been spent, not only by me, but by Shay's parents. There was no way I could back out on the day of. Doing that wasn't even a consideration. I knew I was marrying my best friend, and I had to follow through as planned.

Sadly, my wedding night was also when I started to really wonder if my new husband had a substance issue. Had there been signs prior to that? In retrospect, yes. There was one Christmas party at Villa Blanca when he got blackout drunk and started walking home. This was particularly disturbing, as we didn't live within walking distance. At the time, I didn't dwell on it, because everyone in my group of friends definitely had their vices. Some liked cocaine, some smoked weed, some popped pills of Ecstasy, and Shay preferred his beer with a Vicodin. Honestly, I didn't see a problem with it; I just thought it was his party drug of choice. I'd had a Vicodin with a beer before; it gives you that extra buzz so you don't have to drink as much. I even told this to Lisa, and she said, "What the hell are you talking about?" Clearly, she found it alarming, and she was correct.

Regardless, I didn't think that Shay's penchant for Vicodin and beer meant that he was an addict. I had no idea. I only knew that he liked to let loose and that sometimes it felt over-the-top. When you really love someone, it can be hard to see them clearly, especially if that means having to make tough decisions about your relationship.

For this reason, prior to the wedding, I said to him, "Please do not drink. I want us to remember this night. I don't want you to be wasted and then pass out drunk." He promised me he wouldn't, and I trusted him.

That night, I didn't see him indulge at all, so I assumed he was completely sober, which made me very happy. Seeing Shay honor our big day by abstaining, I began to think that our wedding could still be special despite the hiccups. Then Shay started acting weird. As an aspiring musician, Shay had written a song that he was going to perform for me at the reception. The performance never happened because our wedding coordinator screwed up the timeline.

So, after the wedding, when we went back to one of the casitas we'd rented for the bridal party, Tom Sandoval said, "I'm not going to let the fact that Shay didn't perform at the reception ruin the night. We're going to get everything set up and he's going to sing the song for you." At the time, I was truly touched by what I believed was Tom's thoughtfulness.

Back at the casita, as Shay was doing his thing, I noticed that his eyes were completely glazed over, and he was unsteady on his feet, like he was about to fall down at any moment. I was so confused. Had he gotten that trashed in the short amount of time that Tom was setting things up? Had he taken multiple shots? Popped a pill? It all seemed so unlikely.

A few weeks after the wedding, I got my answer. We were at Tom's house, and he offered us these little blue pills, which he said were Ecstasy. I'd never done Ecstasy before and immediately said I wasn't interested. Shay, appearing perplexed, said, "Wait, that looks like the pill you gave me at the wedding. I thought it was Adderall." We were both in shock. Shay didn't intend to get fucked-up that night. He just wanted an Adderall to stay up later. Of course, I couldn't help but wonder why Shay had to take anything at all, even Adderall.

If I'd known that Tom had given Shay something, I wouldn't have been so upset the morning after the wedding when I was trying to wake Shay up, and he was practically dead to the world. It was super frustrating, but I was able to let it go, even though I didn't know the cause of Shay's hangover at the time. We went away on our honeymoon to Hawaii—where I'd never been before but had always wanted to visit—and despite everything that had gone wrong at the wedding, once we were there, I had an overwhelming sense of bliss. The honeymoon phase is a real thing. I vividly remember, after the pool was closed at our resort, going down to the beach with Shay, reclining on a lounge chair, staring up at the sky, and seeing a shooting star. I wished that I would get everything my heart desired and said a silent little prayer that our marriage would be all that I hoped it would be. I told myself it would.

On the heels of that, my new happy life began as Mrs. Michael Shay, and we got back into the normal swing of things—working and continuing to pursue our dreams in the entertainment industry.

Shortly thereafter, I had to go to the dentist to have a small surgery, for which I was prescribed Vicodin. Since I have a high tolerance for pain, I decided not to take them. However, a few weeks later while cleaning out the medicine cabinet, I noticed the bottle of pills I'd been prescribed was nearly empty. I was so shocked and scared for Shay and for our future together, which transformed into fury.

Did he think I wasn't going to realize? Well, I did. Instantly, I grabbed the bottle, marched into the living room where Shay was sitting, and threw it in his face. I said, "What the fuck? You obviously have a serious issue." Of course, he had some random excuse that I can't even recall. As obvious as his lies seem in hindsight, I believed him, whatever the lie was, as I wasn't yet educated on the patterns of addiction and couldn't imagine Shay hiding something so monumental from me.

Unfortunately, it only got worse from there. There was another time when I was being a good wife and got his truck cleaned for him while he was at work. When I was dropping off the car, I found a massive bottle of pills in the door, which made for an even more massive pit in my stomach. When I confronted him, he said they were someone else's. I let it slide again, because I was still afraid to face the truth.

Later, after one of our visits to my parents' house, they noticed that a few Vicodin had gone missing from my dad's medicine cabinet, which he had a prescription for due to chronic knee issues. My mom said, "Scheana, wake up. You've got to see what's going on here." It might have been clear to the people closest to us, but Shay had told me he was sober, and I was in complete denial. I was furious at my mom for accusing my husband of such a thing. I told myself that maybe my dad had just taken an extra one or two that day. I didn't know. But I certainly didn't think Shay would ever steal from my dad. I assumed that my mom must have been wrong or that the pills were miscounted.

Around this time, I was getting ready to go to New York City to tape *Watch What Happens Live* with Andy Cohen. Whenever I flew to New York, I always took the 6 a.m. flight from LAX so I'd be able to spend some of the day in Manhattan. My car service would arrive at 3:30 in the morning, and I'd stay up all night, not even bothering to pack until 1 a.m. That was when my phone lit up with a Twitter notification from a woman named Becki Butterfly, which said something about wanting to see me that weekend. I assumed it was a fan asking if I was working at SUR, since I was still doing three to five shifts there per week, so I ignored it. Then another notification popped up, and I figured maybe I should check it once I was finished packing so I could see who this person was. When I eventually went to look for it on my Twitter account, the message wasn't there anymore. I thought that was odd; I knew I wasn't crazy and hadn't made up the notification. How did the DM just disappear?

In that moment, I remembered that Shay had logged into his Twitter account on my phone a couple weeks prior, so I switched accounts to his. I saw Becki Butterfly's name, but the messages themselves had been deleted. I went onto her profile and saw that she was a roughly three-hundred-pound BBW (Big Beautiful Woman) porn star. Her profile photo was of her, doggy style, ass to the camera in a thong.

Immediately, I started freaking out. I was thinking, Oh my God, does my husband have some weird fetish that I don't know about? Is he cheating on me? I had intentionally decided to marry a normal person because I was done with unreliable, unfaithful Hollywood types, and now this? I knew Jax was into feet, so maybe Shay was into BBW porn stars. WTF? I considered texting Ariana to get her opinion, but, as much as I knew I could trust her as a friend, it's always risky to confide in fellow cast members, because anything can be revealed on the show when you get in an unexpected fight. Although Ariana was the one cast member I never worried about this with, my anxiety still held me back from telling her.

Instead, I texted my mom. Always one to give solid advice, she wrote, *You're leaving for New York in a couple of hours, go confront him right now. You can't just let this go.* She raised me to be a strong woman, so I'm sure it was hard for her to watch me live in denial.

I walked into the living room, with my heart pounding in my chest, and asked, "Who's Becki Butterfly?" As with his drug use, Shay denied up and down that he knew her, or even that he had any idea what I was talking about. Tired of rolling over, I kept at him. "There's a woman on your Twitter account, a porn star, who's DMing to see you this weekend. How convenient that I'm going out of town. What is this?" I was so confused. And, again, he totally deflected, saying, "Are you kidding? Do you actually think I would be interested in someone like that? She's just a fan who asked if we were around this weekend, because she wants to meet us." Still baffled and suspicious, I asked, "Then why are you deleting the messages? You could have simply replied that I wasn't going to be at SUR. You're hiding something." He shook his head, and insisted that I was being "crazy." He'd perfected the art of gaslighting. Still, I had to head to the airport for my flight to New York, and I wanted so badly to believe him, so I let it go.

Our first year of marriage went on like that, as if we were stuck on the worst roller coaster of all time. There were some bright spots, like these mini-getaway trips we'd take to Las Vegas, which always had a certain sheen since we'd rekindled our relationship there. But on one of those usually fun trips, we got into a huge fight. I can't even remember what it was about, but I do recall that Shay threw his phone at the wall in the hotel room, and the screen shattered. I had to fly from Vegas to New York for another *Watch What Happens Live* appearance that was booked last-minute, and Shay was hitching a ride with some friends back to LA. Now that he had a broken phone, my anxiety had me in a full panic. As mad as I was at Shay, I couldn't help but worry about him. What if he couldn't get home safely? What if something happened and he couldn't reach me because of his shattered phone? What if he was in a car accident? I was ready to travel across the country, and I needed to be able to make sure my husband got home safely.

Thankfully, my sister had an extra iPhone, so I told Shay to stop in Azusa on his way home and borrow it from her. He was on my phone plan, so I needed to be present for him to buy a new one, which I said we'd do once I was back. Shay agreed and Cortney kindly said that he could hang on to the phone until we sorted everything out.

A few weeks later, Cortney—who was seventeen at this point—and her friend were at my place in Park La Brea, which happened pretty regularly. And Katie Maloney was there, too. We'd gotten closer over the seasons, and Katie was doing my sister's friend's hair.

Cortney and I were on her computer online shopping when, all of a sudden, a text message popped up on her screen from a cute Hispanic girl with pink streaks in her hair. Cortney told me she had no idea who this woman was, and also that she'd been getting some of Shay's messages, since he didn't set up his own iCloud after borrowing her phone. I said, "Hold up, I don't know who this girl is. Why is she sending my husband a photo?"

We opened the message chain, which only went back a week. You could tell it was half of a conversation, so it was clear he was deleting messages, but we were able to scroll a bit. We saw a message from Shay saying, "You on top of me sounds really good right now."

I was heartbroken and furious at the same time. Not to mention that I couldn't hide it or protect him, even if I'd wanted to, because my sister was a witness. This forced me to finally face the truth.

I called Shay on the spot and started screaming at him at the top of my lungs.

He told me it was a fan he'd met while bartending at Mixology and that she was visiting LA with her mom. They'd started following each other on Twitter, and then he gave her his number. He said it was just an emotional affair, never physical, because she lived in Florida and was married. As hurt and humiliated as I was, my pride won out over every other emotion. In order to save face, especially in front of Cortney and Katie, I decided to let it go yet again. I was too embarrassed to admit that he was talking to someone else behind my back, so I decided to believe him when he said it would never happen again.

At this point, we were filming season five of *Vanderpump*

Rules, and Ariana and I were having a conversation for a scene in my bedroom. I remember our producer saying, "Scheana, I feel you're off. It's like you're hiding something. We're not getting the full story here. What is it?"

The producer was right. Ariana could tell, too, so I had to spill something. I just wasn't able to tell the truth in that moment. I envisioned what the reaction would be—You deserve this because of what you did to Brandi. So, instead of being honest, I shared that Shay had an addiction issue. I knew it was an extremely relatable struggle that many people could understand. I was being honest; even if it wasn't the most destructive problem in our marriage, it was at the very least simmering beneath his emotional cheating.

This was the first time I'd covered up a partner's indiscretion for the cameras, but it sadly wouldn't be the last. What I've learned about myself since then is that when I try to conceal my truth, I can't veil my emotions. They come out one way or another, misplaced and ill-received by the audience. At that time, I just felt like I needed to do my job, which was paying all of our bills. This meant I had to give the show a kernel, and they took it gladly.

By the end of the season, we were taping at Katie and Tom's wedding, and I was lying through my teeth to everyone, saying how happy I was with Shay. How I was getting butterflies all over again, and that we were back on track and better than before. I think some people bought it and some people didn't. I really did love him so much. He was my number one person—my past, my present, and I hoped my future. I took our wedding vows seriously and refused to give up. I felt like if I kept faking it, maybe our relationship would actually get better on its own.

It took a couple of other strange things going down to make carrying on feel impossible.

The first of which was one night when Shay didn't come home, and I couldn't reach him. He'd been at his music studio, but a friend told me he'd left and had no idea where he'd gone. Of course I got scared. Who wouldn't? Again, he could have been in a car accident or been injured in some way. I had my friend Courtney Berman drive around the streets looking for him, while my mom and I called every hospital and police station.

It wasn't until eight the following morning that he showed up at our door completely disheveled. He said he'd had to walk back from the studio because he'd locked his phone, his car key, and his wallet in the studio. That explanation sounded pretty suspicious. Couldn't he have borrowed someone's phone? Even a stranger's? It was so bizarre. His story wasn't adding up, but I couldn't prove that he was lying.

A few weeks later, Shay and I hosted a Halloween party at SUR, in partnership with a French champagne brand called Freixenet. I didn't know it at the time, but this was the beginning of the last week of our marriage. Shay had performed with his band at the party, and the next day they were in the studio returning the equipment. He texted me that evening to say, *I'm about to head home soon. Do you want me to pick up anything for you at the store?* It was 11 p.m., but I was hungry, so I replied, *If you're really leaving soon, call me on your way, and I'll let you know what I want. If not, I don't need anything.* He said okay and added that he'd be in touch.

Two hours later, I hadn't heard from him, and—given his track record—I was getting worried. After what had happened the last time, I'd made him start sharing his location with me so I could see that his phone was still at the studio. Yet, when I called his band members, they said they'd already left, so he was there alone. And, again, he never came home.

The following day, I checked his location once more to find that he was at his parents' house, and right after that, he turned his phone off. This shady behavior prompted me to log in to our joint bank account, where I saw that roughly $6,000—all the money I'd set aside to pay our rent and bills for the month—had been drained.

Frantically, I tried calling and texting him, but he wouldn't answer. Finally, I got a hold of his brother, who said he was safe, with his family, and didn't want to speak to me. I thought, What the hell is going on? I had to reach out to my business manager to transfer money from my personal account so I could make rent, and then I looked at my Amex account (which he had a card under), to find that another $600 had been spent at Top Shop Man. I didn't know if it was him or if he'd lost the card, but I was livid.

A full week went by with no word from Shay. I was doing interviews for season five of *VPR*, and production knew something was fishy. As much as I wanted to keep it all under wraps, I confessed that Shay hadn't been home for days and, despite the fact that we'd ended season five in August 2016 on a happy note with Schwartz and Katie getting married, and Sandoval and Schwartz opening a restaurant called TomTom, they decided to pick up cameras in October for a new finale. If I'm being honest, I felt like my marriage with Shay was over at this point, but I wasn't ready to fully accept that yet and wanted to try every last effort to make it work.

I ended up filming a scene with Lisa, where I opened up

about Shay's issues and told her that I wasn't sure if he was coming back. This also happened to coincide with my uncle's best friend, whom I was very close with and considered another uncle, passing away. At his funeral, my entire family was asking where my husband was, and I had no idea what to say. Even for Shay, skipping that event was an all-time low.

Not to mention that there had been leaks in production, which is typical, and *TMZ* was reporting that Shay was on a bender, so Shay's family hated me because they felt like I'd exposed him despite all I'd done to protect him over the years. I actually believed in the vows we'd taken—for better or worse, till death do us part. Shay obviously did not. I'm sure being married to me wasn't always a walk in the park, but I genuinely loved Shay and wanted us to work.

The day after my uncle's best friend's funeral, Shay finally came by our apartment to have a conversation with me. It was so awkward, but he did apologize and say he wanted to make things work. Pathetically, I slept with him and said I'd try to hold our marriage together. I so badly wanted to avoid divorce because of the negative associations with it. I also still loved him. Both my pride and my heart definitely got in the way of doing what, at that point, was obviously the right thing.

I told him that I was having lunch with one of the *VPR* producers and that they asked to film us making up. He agreed. This was on a Sunday, and we were set to tape on Wednesday. I wouldn't say I felt great about it, but I was prepared to attempt to patch things up. As I said, for better or worse.

That Monday, it was the premiere of season five, and Kristen was hosting a viewing party at her house. I was at her apartment, making my famous enchiladas, and my castmates were asking how things were going with me and Shay. I told them that we were hoping to move forward, and that I believed things were going to be okay. I felt like it was my last chance to make our marriage work. Everyone seemed very happy for us and was very supportive, except Jax.

The two of us got in a huge fight that night. I left to call an Uber home, but Kristen begged me to come back and said Jax would leave instead. But, before he could, I made a comment to him about how poorly he treated Brittany Cartwright, his then girlfriend who began appearing on *VPR* in Season 4. He shot back with "At least she hasn't left me like your husband left you." It was such a typical asshole comment from Jax, when he knew I was clearly struggling. I was *married*. Shay wasn't just a boyfriend I could easily break up with and move on. We lived together. We shared a bank account. We were building a life together.

To make matters worse, my friend "A" pulled me into the kitchen and said, "I saw the *TMZ* report about Shay's supposed bender. I just want to make sure your issues have nothing to do with the Adderall he's been buying from me." I said, "Come again?" My head was spinning. He replied, "He's been buying it for the last few months. He said the band members needed it for when they were in the studio late to help them stay awake. He also wanted it when you went to that festival not long before Halloween, but I'd run out."

Right then, I had a flashback to the concert series we were at with my parents in Indio, California, called Desert Trip (aka the Oldchella festival). The performers were the Rolling Stones, Bob Dylan, Paul McCartney, Neil Young, Roger Waters, and the Who. The whole *VPR* cast was there, too. My parents, Shay, and I stayed at a friend's house on the PGA West golf course.

While Shay was "sober" at the time, I'd brought beer and vodka for everyone else. On the first day of the festival, I noticed that a large portion of the handle of vodka was gone. I thought that was strange because my dad was more of a beer guy, and I'd only had one drink. Immediately, I asked Shay if he was drinking again and he said no. I explained that there was a lot of vodka missing, and he claimed that when he was grabbing something out of the cabinet, the cap hadn't been secured properly, and he'd knocked it over and spilled it.

I was a little bit skeptical, but also in denial. I wanted so badly to believe my husband. Yet, when I told my mom what had happened, she said, "Scheana, first of all, you're being naïve. Second of all, do you really think if Shay had spilled the vodka, he would have quietly cleaned it up and not said anything?" I knew she had a point, but I ignored it.

After that, when we were at the actual festival, Shay was unusually irritable. I didn't realize what was going on in that moment, but when "A" told me he'd been out of Adderall at the time, I realized that Shay must have been going through withdrawal. If he'd had his pills, he probably wouldn't have drunk the vodka. But he obviously needed some kind of buzz.

Another thing that occurred to me was a $600 charge that had been coming out of our joint account every three weeks. When I'd asked Shay about it, he'd said he was paying his parents back for the thousands of dollars of floral arrangements they'd purchased for our wedding. I didn't even think to question it or to confirm with his mom. I said to "A," "By any chance does the Adderall he's been getting from you cost $600?" Sure enough, the answer was yes.

I was in shock, even though I had every reason not to be.

But I didn't confront Shay immediately. Instead, I waited until Wednesday and hatched a plan. The producers of *VPR* thought they were going to be filming a reconciliation scene, but I had a very different idea in mind. I was going to challenge Shay with the information I'd gleaned from "A" and give him every opportunity to come clean. If he did, I was going to send him to rehab. I was willing to invest the last penny I had into his recovery, because he was my husband, and I wanted him to be okay. When you love someone, you're willing to go to the ends of the earth.

The reason I decided to do it on camera was because we'd already addressed that he "left me" and disappeared for a week on the show. And we needed to complete the narrative for the new finale. I truly hoped it would be a story of us working things out and coming back together.

According to plan, once the cameras were rolling, I afforded Shay the chance to tell the truth about his addiction. I said, "Listen, I'm not accusing *you* of still taking drugs, but have you picked up any form of pills for someone else? Maybe you're the middleman?" He said no, that wasn't the case. I added, "So, to confirm, you're telling me that in the last three months, you have not bought one pill for yourself or anyone else?" He doubled down and said he had not, which was the final straw for me. I knew that if Shay could lie to my face that convincingly, he wasn't someone I could stay married to, much less eventually have children with. We were done.

I said I wanted a divorce, right there on tape, and my producer's jaw dropped open. It was a major plot twist that he didn't see coming, and he actually told me later that he thought I was a cold-hearted bitch in that moment—even though I was actually heartbroken and defeated—until he understood the context behind my reaction.

Cut to Shay at our apartment, packing his bags, while sad music played in the background. That was the official end of season five, my two-year marriage, and our seven-year relationship.

Once I'd made the decision to leave Shay, I wanted to be done with everything as quickly as possible. I had $100,000 in my business account, and I informed Shay that if he agreed to sign divorce papers immediately, I would split it with him.

Predictably, Shay was on board with that plan. But the day of the signing, he said he was too tired to drive to our appointment and tried to get out of it. In turn, I reminded him that I was paying *all* the attorney fees, and it was a holiday, so he needed to get his ass in the car and drive to LA, which he did. We met at my attorney's office and signed the papers. He took the money, and we said goodbye. Our attorney said that it was the most amicable divorce she'd ever done.

To my surprise, Shay did attend the *VPR* reunion that year, but we didn't speak for at least another year after that, when we finally had a conversation that gave us some closure to our marriage. We both recognized that we'd hurt each other. And I apologized to him for how I'd handled the end of our relationship, specifically about how I discussed his addiction on television. I also said I was sorry that he had to find out at the reunion that I was seeing someone else so soon after we broke up. I believe Shay really heard me and understood. We both cried and felt at peace. And, from that point on, we were in a good place.

As a result, I was comfortable reaching out to him when his mother passed away in March 2023, but I sadly couldn't go to the funeral because it was the same day as that season's *VPR* reunion.

I texted him that morning at 7:43 a.m. and said, *Sending you and your family so much love today.* He replied, *Thank you so much. Good luck. Reunions suck.*

I truly do wish Shay the best, and I'm proud of the work he has done on himself over the years. I've always thought and still think that he'll be the best father one day. Unfortunately, the timing wasn't right for us, and we weren't meant to be in the long run. He is an incredible person with a huge heart and love for his family, and I know he'll make the right girl very happy one day.

8

IT'S COMPLICATED

With both my marriage to Shay and season five behind me, I was amazingly still in relationship mode. I wasn't ready to be single again at thirty-two. I wanted to be married and have children one day, and I felt like it had to be pretty soon.

The week after the papers were signed, I reconnected with a guy named Rob, whom I'd met in my early twenties, after I was with Jesse Metcalfe. Rob had worked as a doorman at a place called Joseph's, where I'd go on Monday nights, and which was where I met Jesse. At first, I didn't talk to Rob, but eventually, since I was there every week, we became friendly and exchanged numbers. Not long after, he asked me out.

For our first date back then, he took me to Disneyland. We'd been there all day, when I realized he hadn't tried to kiss me yet. Rob was the kind of person who always had to wait for the perfect moment to do anything. I really wanted him to kiss me, but every time I assumed it was going to happen, he'd pull away. I was thinking, What is this shit? You bring me on a date to one of my favorite places and refuse to make a move? I wasn't used to that. Thankfully, when the fireworks went off at the end of the night, we finally locked lips. He wanted it to be a magical moment, and it was. In retrospect, I think that his whole playing-hard-to-get act was what hooked me.

To be clear, Rob wasn't my boyfriend at that time, but we did have an instant, deep connection. And the sex was amazing. Actually, I was sort of obsessed and would have done anything to hold on to him, but I was young and he wouldn't commit to me, and I was nearly ready to start settling down. As a result, things didn't work out between us.

Fast-forward to my wedding day with Shay, when I was worried that I had cold feet, I recall wondering how my life would have played out if I'd ended up with Rob. We had so much in common, from the way we were raised by single moms with a very present stepfather and the fact that we were both Tauruses, to our shared values and parenting ideals. Sometimes it felt like we were the same person. Rob and I never disagreed about anything, although he did have a commitment phobia. As I write this, he's forty-two and still single.

Toward the end of my marriage to Shay—around September 2016—I was at a music festival in San Diego called KAABOO, with my sister and my friend Colin (who reminded me so much of the Collin who'd taken his own life). My sister broke off to go see Chainsmokers, and Colin and I went to see Aerosmith, when all of a sudden I felt the presence of a tall guy standing next to me. He said, "Has anyone ever told you that you look like Scheana from *Vanderpump Rules*?" I said, "Oh, yeah, I'm Scheana." Then I looked up to find Rob smiling down at me. I couldn't believe it. I hadn't seen him in years. He leaned over to give me a big hug, and immediately I knew I still had feelings for him, despite being married to Shay. In light of this realization, I whispered to Colin, "You are not leaving my side for the rest of the night." I didn't care how many bad things Shay had done in our relationship; I wasn't a cheater. I also wondered, in that moment, if I would feel this way about Rob right now if my marriage were perfectly happy and had no signs of betrayal. I guess I'll never really know.

That night my sister and I went back to our hotel, and I received a text from Rob saying, *It was really good to see you. Hope things have been well.* I replied with *Good to see you too, everything's not the best, but I'll let you know how it shakes out.* For the next month, while things with Shay got increasingly worse, all I could think about was Rob.

So, once Shay and I were divorced, I made plans to see Rob, slept with him, and dove in headfirst. I was ready to be with someone I could trust and rely on and start a family with, even though Rob, his friends, and my friends were concerned that I hadn't really processed my split from Shay and everything I'd been through with him. They thought it was way too soon to be moving on. But I assured them that my marriage had been over for so long, and I was fine. This probably wasn't the case, because when Rob ultimately broke up with me and crushed my heart, I then felt the weight of my divorce and our subsequent breakup. It was a double heartache.

The main issue with Rob, aside from his fear of commitment,

was that he wanted nothing to do with *Vanderpump Rules*. Despite how much I loved being on *VPR* and working with my friends, I was also super into Rob. Not only did we have a deep trust and intense connection, but Rob had also invited me to cohost episodes of his show, *This Is LA*. I still dreamed of one day being a TV host, and I loved cohosting with him. We had great chemistry, and those shows were so fun to tape together. It felt like we had similar dreams and a shared ambition, and I imagined us traveling the world as life and business partners. So, I offered to quit *VPR* for him. I'd done it for five years, and I was prepared to make that sacrifice. But, before I could, Rob said that he wouldn't let me walk away from the show for him. Thank God! That was probably the best thing he did for me.

Eventually, Rob said if he had to be involved with *VPR* in order to stay with me, he would. So we met with the producers to discuss his level of participation, even though he really didn't like that he would have no editing control over how he was portrayed. That was his biggest hesitation.

Soon after he signed on, I was filming a scene with Kristen and Brittany when they sat me down for a seemingly serious conversation. They informed me that one of their friends who worked at a Mexican restaurant called Toca Madera in West Hollywood said that Rob had come in recently and was making out with one of the hostesses there. I knew it was bullshit because Rob was very weird about PDA, even with me. I said, "You're telling me that my boyfriend, who barely kisses me in public, just walked into a restaurant, picked up a hostess, twirled her around, and then started kissing her? You expect me to believe that?" They thought I was in denial.

I realized that this was exactly why he didn't want to be a

part of the show. Once something is said on camera, whether it's true or not, it's out there. After that scene, I told my producer that I was going to call Rob, with my microphone off. I felt I at least owed him that. In hindsight, maybe he did make out with that hostess. Perhaps that was why he was reluctant to be on television as my boyfriend. I'll never know, but I stuck to my guns.

When I reached Rob by phone, he was out of town with his friend Jake Pavelka, the former Bachelor. I shared the gossip with him, and he promptly lost his shit. I felt him completely shut down. He confirmed what I already knew, which was that his fear about being tied to *VPR* had come true. And the following day when I picked him up at the airport, he was so cold to me.

Thankfully, he compartmentalized our issues and didn't want to talk about them, so we decided to meet his business partner at a pool party at the Mondrian hotel. It was a Sunday, and we weren't filming. We figured we might as well let loose, down a few drinks, and have fun to release some of the pressure.

That was the day I met Janet Caperna. Initially, she was a fan of the show, and we had a mutual friend, so she didn't seem like a complete stranger. We ended up getting really drunk together and taking way too many pictures. Janet told me that she was leaving a marriage with some similar problems to mine and Shay's, and we bonded over that. To this day, we're still super close. Nothing brings two people together like sharing the same struggles.

From there, I hoped everything was going to be fine with me and Rob. It seemed like he had moved on, and filming picked back up with his involvement. I insisted to the rest of the cast that him making out with the hostess was bullshit. And then, standard Scheana, I started overcompensating by talking about how amazing he was all the time. I couldn't have the world thinking he was a cheater, because once the show aired, I knew he would break up with me if I did nothing to protect him. And I certainly couldn't go from a failed marriage to a failed relationship.

Two weeks after we wrapped, Rob asked me to come over to his place. I'll never forget that he had his fantasy football draft going on, so I sat there hanging out with his dog, twiddling my damn thumbs, for two hours while he picked his team. Finally, he closed his computer, looked at me, and said, "This isn't working." He went on to explain that he'd been doing me a favor by staying with me through season six, because he didn't want me to have to deal with a breakup story line. I said, "Are you serious? If you knew this three months ago, why did you put me through a whole season with you? Every time I said I love you on camera, and you didn't say it back, I looked so dumb." I guess he didn't care, despite what he said to me or wanted to believe about himself.

As it happened, I was about to go to Atlanta the next day with Brittany, because she and Jax had split up that season. He cheated on her with her "friend" Faith, so we were primed for a girls' getaway. I said to Rob, "You're really going to dump me the day before I leave town? Are you stupid?" Apparently, he didn't think so, because he did it anyway. And, while Brittany and I were able to let loose a bit in Atlanta, we also spent some of the trip consoling each other.

Pathetically, even though Rob broke my heart, I was so desperate to keep him around that I continued sleeping with him for four months after that. There was just such an appeal about him, partly because he'd rejected me, which made me want him even more. I also loved his family, specifically his mom. She was so amazing that I still keep in touch with her. She was a woman I could really see as my mother-in-law. His dad and siblings were awesome, too. It was a family I wanted to be a part of and could imagine a future with. I knew that Rob and I had the same values and that we would raise kids the same way. I wanted that life so badly, especially since it hadn't worked out with Shay. And, again, I had so much pride that I didn't want to admit I couldn't keep a marriage and then I couldn't keep a boyfriend.

The worst part was that after one of the times we slept together postbreakup, he rolled over in my bed the next morning, cuddled me, and told me he loved me. It was the first time he'd ever said it and truly meant it. I was thinking, What is wrong with you? Why are you telling me this now when you don't want to be with me? It was so manipulative and so fucked-up; it really did a number on me.

Profession of love aside, Rob decided to take a solo trip to Italy to find himself. I thought, Screw Rob; I'm done with him. I wasn't going to wait around for him, as hurt as I was. As per usual, I eased my pain by turning to a bunch of new guys, namely four men who'd been on *The Bachelorette*, who all lived in a house together in Venice, California.

One day when we were hanging out, one of them told me about this very spiritual event in Las Vegas called RiSE, which is a festival where they release thousands of lanterns into the sky. He invited me and my friends, so off I went with him to Vegas. I was thankful to have a rebound guy who was treating me nicely. That is, until the night after RiSE, when he went to a gentleman's club called Sapphire and left with a stripper named Sierra. It was almost comical. There I was rebounding with a guy who'd ditched me for a fucking stripper. That would be my luck.

Meanwhile, I was getting phone calls and texts from Rob in Italy, who was watching my social media stories and scolding me for partying in Vegas. He said, If you really want to be with me, how could you be doing this? I know you're sleeping with another guy. The irony was the guy he thought I was sleeping with was the only one of the four I hadn't hooked up with!

I was so over the whole thing with Rob and the guys from *The Bachelorette*. I thought, Fuck all of them, I want to do something fun and for myself. The next day in Vegas, I saw a taxi on the strip that had an advertisement with my friends Jai Rodriguez and Kendra Wilkinson's photo on it. They were doing a show together called *Sex Tips for Straight Women from a Gay Man*. So, I texted them and asked if I could come to their show that night, and they said yes. The show was so funny, and I ended up getting dinner with them after. It was early October, and they told me that their residency was wrapping up at the beginning of January and suggested that I should take over for Kendra. It was definitely intriguing to think about being onstage every night, performing live on the Las Vegas strip, and having my face on billboards and cab tops for my acting skills. What a dream! Even after being on *VPR* for six years, I still wanted to be an actress and thought this seemed like a perfect opportunity. Yet, I couldn't imagine uprooting my life in LA to move to Vegas. Still, Kendra said I should consider it and that she would give my information to the producers.

Later that evening, I was hanging out with my sister's

boyfriend, Justice, and his family for his birthday, telling them about the show opportunity. They were like, you have to do it. Vegas is such a cool place to live, even if it's only temporary. Of course, I had to audition for the part. And what were the chances that I'd actually get it? What was the harm in just trying? So I taped my audition and sent it off.

Not long after that, I received a call from the producers of *Sex Tips for Straight Women from a Gay Man*, saying that I'd booked the role. They needed me in Vegas in one month for the photo shoot for the promotional materials and billboards, and then I had to move there in December for the show's run. I couldn't have been more thrilled. It felt like exactly the fresh start I needed and a very cool opportunity to do something totally new to me and completely outside of reality television. Maybe it would even lead to other acting gigs.

It did take some convincing with the producers at *VPR* and from the tone in Lisa's voice, I could tell she did not want me to do it, that she thought it would be a bad look for me to participate in something outside of LA and also not work at the restaurants for a while. But I thought it was so ridiculous and unfair, because the majority of the cast no longer worked at the restaurants. I was one of the only people who still showed up, while everyone else got to live their lives. I wasn't even collecting tips from the pool anymore. It always felt like I was bound to SUR and, if I quit, I could be fired from the show.

I said I could fly back every Tuesday night after my Vegas appearance, record my podcast—which I was about to launch—on Wednesday, work at the restaurants Wednesday night, and then return to Vegas Thursday morning, for nearly six months. Eventually, everyone agreed to let me go.

On December 25, 2017, I was off. My sister and I had Christmas morning with our parents, then I packed up and drove to Vegas with my cats, Penny Lane and Salem, whom I'd adopted a few months before I married Shay. I started rehearsals that week and performed in my inaugural show the first week in January. Over the course of the following six months, many of my friends and family came to see me, including Brittany, Janet, James Kennedy, Tom Sandoval, and, obviously, my parents. Ariana made it out for my very final show, and it was a night to celebrate! The funny thing is that even the guy from *The Bachelorette* who left me for the stripper came to support me—and I realized if he hadn't left me, I never would've gone to see the show and ended up in the role. I thanked him that night. Katie, Stassi, Kristen, and Lala Kent did not attend, which was particularly disappointing because Lala was in Vegas a couple of times. I was really hurt that they didn't support me, even though we weren't as close at the time. Still, I thought that with roughly 160 shows, they could have made it to one…if only to make fun of me!

Rob was also there for opening night, which made me happy. But by that point I'd come to the realization that he was never going to prioritize our relationship, so I told him that I couldn't see him or talk to him anymore. I didn't want to do the same song and dance forever. I had to go cold turkey and live the single life yet again. Otherwise, I knew I'd keep pining after him.

Those months were the exact reset I needed. Single Scheana thrived in Vegas. Whether I was on stage at my own show or at *Thunder from Down Under*, *Magic Mike*, or *Chippendales*, I was having the best time. Honestly, I would have extended my residency if I could have. I loved doing *Sex Tips for Straight Women from a Gay Man*. The feeling of being onstage every night, acting and dancing, making people laugh, and meeting fans was so rewarding. It was a dream come true, not only to be onstage but to bring joy to the thousands of people who came to see the show. Also, the producers put me up in a beautiful apartment in Vegas, which was hard to beat.

But sadly, I couldn't stay. *VPR* had been picked up for a seventh season, and I needed to go back to LA to film. Being in Las Vegas helped me realize that I didn't want to return to the Park La Brea community, where I had nothing but memories of Shay and Rob in my apartment. I needed a fresh start, take two.

My mom, amazing and supportive woman that she is, helped me find a new apartment in Marina del Rey, ordered me all new furniture, and—along with my best guy friend, Adam—moved all of my stuff in for me before the end of the residency. When I arrived home from Vegas, I drove straight to my new place overlooking the water, and the entire apartment was set up. It felt like things were finally taking shape.

I was refreshed and ready for season seven. I thought it was going to be so fun to film the show completely single for the first time, even though I was the only one without a partner. Lala was with Randall Emmett, Katie was with Tom Schwartz, Tom Sandoval was with Ariana, Stassi was with Beau Clark, James was with Raquel, and Kristen was with Brian Carter. I suppose, for that reason, it ended up being the furthest thing from fun. I felt totally alone. I was fine with going home and sleeping by myself—that wasn't the problem. Most days, I was living my best life and genuinely enjoying it. However, when the cameras were up, it was obvious that I didn't fit in. And I definitely didn't feel like I had a number one the way everyone else did. Maybe that was why I started sleeping with Adam. We did have a great connection, but it was a terrible idea because it ended up ruining our friendship, which I regret.

Beyond these dynamics, one of the strangest elements of season seven was that Ariana and Stassi somehow became closer while I was in Vegas. I use the word *strange*, because Ariana never really liked Stassi. I wondered what happened to change things in the near six months I was gone. Suddenly Ariana and Stassi were doing things like dressing in matching costumes for their birthdays, both June 24. I felt like their relationship was another punishment for my being away for so long.

To make matters worse, I knew that Kristen had been demoted for season seven, and—since my own contract was only for seven years—I was afraid that my future for season eight was also in jeopardy.

And, guess what? I was absolutely right.

I just didn't know it yet.

9

HOW TO BE SINGLE

With season seven wrapped and airing, I went to New York to do press for *VPR*, which included what was sure to be a killer appearance on *Watch What Happens Live*. In the clubhouse it's always a good time with fun vibes. While I was finishing glam, I got a call from one of the *VPR* producers, Jeremiah Smith. As soon as I saw his name, I was concerned. Jeremiah didn't call unless it was important. And, with all my anxieties about my place on the show still swirling, I had a gut feeling that it was bad news.

When I picked up the phone, he told me that Bill Langworthy and Alex Baskin, two executives on the show, wanted me to come in for a meeting the next day. Getting summoned by higher-ups is *never* a good thing, especially when conversations for the next season (in this case, eight) are starting, so I knew that my instincts were correct. Something was wrong.

I told Jeremiah that I was in Manhattan doing press to promote the show, which I was surprised he didn't realize, and that I wouldn't be able to make it in the following day. Then I asked directly, "What's the meeting about?" He was evasive and kept insisting that it wasn't a big deal, and I should just let them know when I was back in LA. Something still seemed fishy, so I asked once more what the meeting was about. Again, he said not to worry about it, which of course made me worry about it even more, especially because I knew that Kristen had already been demoted.

As soon as we hung up, I called Alex and said, "I've got five minutes until I go on live television for *your* show, and I just got a call asking me for a meeting. I need you to tell me what's going on." I knew I couldn't play it cool if I didn't have answers before we started rolling. Alex replied, "All I can say is that it's not a meeting you'll look forward to." I asked, "Is it similar to what happened with Kristen? Is that what you guys are going to do to me?" He said yes, confirming my suspicion.

A lump formed in my throat. I was sad and confused, not to mention pissed off. Why me? Why now? I'd given so much to the show from the beginning, not to mention how I'd just spent six months flying back and forth to Las Vegas to keep up my filming schedule, and I felt completely unappreciated. Sensing my disappointment and anxiety, Alex said, "Just try to relax and go do *Watch What Happens Live*. We'll talk when you get back."

Relax?! Not possible. I was freaking out. I loved the show, and the money didn't hurt, either. Suddenly it seemed like my future was at stake.

I pulled Andy Cohen aside and explained to him what was going on. I thought he might have some influence, and he would always tell me how he was rooting for me, so I hoped he might want to help. At first, he said, "You know I don't work on your show. I have no say whatsoever, but I can tell you that if this is what they're doing, they're making a huge mistake. You are *Vanderpump Rules*."

I couldn't believe what I was hearing. How could Andy Cohen have no influence over casting decisions for *VPR*? I was sobbing. He looked at me sympathetically and said, "Listen, we're a few minutes from air. I need you to get your shit together, make great TV, and show everyone that you deserve your spot on the show." I nodded, knowing he was right—the best thing I could possibly do was demonstrate to the execs what a big mistake they were making—even though I could feel the panic rising in my chest. I downed multiple Moscow Mules and hit my weed pen in an attempt to ease my angst and then emotionally blacked out from all the stress.

Thankfully, Carl Radke, from *Summer House*, was the other guest on *WWHL* with me. He'd joined *Summer House* as part of a backdoor pilot episode of *VPR*, and both of our moms were bartending at *WWHL* that night. Since Carl and I were friends, it felt like a safe space for me, so I was able to calm down a bit and have fun despite all the anxiety I was feeling.

The next day, my mom and I spent the afternoon walking around New York and having lunch with Carl and his mom in the West Village. It was the most beautiful day in the city—the sun was shining and there wasn't a cloud in the sky. It was so warm, we didn't even need coats. As we walked to the restaurant, I looked up at the sky and thought, I could totally live here. At lunch, I ordered an Aperol spritz and a salad and reminisced with Carl and our moms about our favorite moments together, which only made the day feel more perfect.

I later confided in my mom that maybe I was done with *VPR* and should move to New York to start a new chapter. Living in Manhattan had always been a dream of mine, and perhaps the timing was finally right. I was seriously considering it, but I realized that such a major change, on a whim, with no new job to speak of, was probably not the right decision.

So, I returned to LA, met with production, and found out that I was being officially demoted for season eight. Alex said, "I'm sorry, Scheana. This is not my call. But we don't want to lose you; we still value you. You're the glue that ties SUR to our new cast members." He also shared that after season eight, they were planning to do a spin-off show (which later became *The Valley*) and that if I stayed, I'd be part of both. It was clear that I wouldn't have that opportunity if I left.

The demotion was particularly disappointing because I was in a good place with everyone. The problem with our show was that we weren't like the *Jersey Shore* cast, who had banded together to protect their salaries—my castmates were not willing to unite in protecting one another. I do recall that Sandoval called Alex and went to bat on my behalf, but he was the only one. His attempt to help me was lost on production, though not forgotten by me. It was things like this that made our friendship special back then.

Meanwhile, I'd just put down a 20 percent deposit on a home in Palm Springs that I was in escrow for. I felt comfortable doing that because I'd asked the producers if they thought the show was going to be renewed for season eight. They'd said it wasn't a guarantee but that they strongly believed it would be. If not for that reassurance, I never would have initiated buying a new house. And regardless of whether or not the show was continuing, I wouldn't have done it if I'd known I was being demoted.

I was also an easy target. I let them walk all over me—for example, when I signed on to the show, the network said they might include my creative pursuits. And then I barely put up a fight when they didn't feature *Sex Tips for Straight Women from a Gay Man* on *VPR* or take any interest in my podcast, which was doing very well, as I'd interviewed several celebrities in my first year. Every day, no matter what I had to deal with, I would show up and do my job with a smile on my face. What choice did I have? The job was paying my bills. Where else was I going to make as much a day consistently for ten weeks?

They knew I wouldn't and couldn't quit. Of course, if Stassi had been demoted, she'd have resigned on the spot. But I didn't have the guts to be that bold, because I didn't feel confident in myself at that time, whereas Stassi always did. Things with the group and with the show never seemed to work out in my favor, so I had a lot of self-doubt.

With that understanding, I changed my outlook. I was determined to make the best of a shitty situation, and knew that the only person I was in control of was myself. I viewed season eight as a bridge to having gigs on two different shows, *VPR* and the spin-off.

The summer of 2019 we filmed season eight. Before we started, Lisa informed me that she was really counting on me to bring the new servers/cast members at SUR into the fold and to help tie in their story lines to the show. She made me feel like I had an integral role, despite my devaluation, and—of course—I accepted my position.

So I plastered a smile on my face and was ready to welcome

the new girls to *VPR* with open arms, one of whom was Charli Burnett. We both lived on the west side and had a lot of things in common, including that we were half Mexican and half white, so I saw her as a younger version of me. We hit it off immediately. I felt very protective of her and tried to guide her. Charli wasn't friends with anyone at SUR and I wanted to show her the ropes. I had so much fun with her when she first started. Despite my demotion, I was still a main character, and that was the energy I needed to continue to give, and working with Charli made it easy.

As for Dayna Kathan, I met her briefly at a party at Katie's house when the season was starting. I definitely didn't vibe with her right off the bat. Our personalities were very different. She had more of a dark, dry sense of humor and was one of those girls who knows she's cool. In all honesty, maybe I was jealous of her in the beginning. She had that season one confidence that I had lost. Dayna walked into the party like she belonged, whereas I felt like an outsider around all of *my* friends, because I'd been demoted. It made me insecure about my place in the group, even though no one treated me any differently or like I was inferior. It was still painful to be singled out.

Dayna had just begun working at TomTom with Max Boyens, who was the manager there, and whom I'd dated for about five weeks between seasons seven and eight. That first weekend of season eight, I had an off-camera trip to Palm Springs planned with Janet and a group of my friends. Max was coming as well, and when we were chatting about the trip beforehand, Dayna overheard that we were going together. I'd learned, secondhand, that she and Max had started "talking" when she joined the staff at TomTom, but since Max never said anything to me, I thought nothing of it. I had no idea that she was interested in him romantically.

So, we went to Palm Springs and had a crazy fun night filled with drinks, games of Truth or Dare and another called Pizza Box that Janet made up and used to play back in Ohio; it was similar to Truth or Dare, except it involved flipping a coin and coming up with rules for people that were always dares.

When it came time for bed, Max got in mine. The next morning, Max and I fooled around a little. Did I initiate it? Sure, but he was a very willing participant, until he wasn't and said we shouldn't go any further. When we got back, he told everyone that I was trying to come on to him, and that he didn't want me. That pissed me off, because it sparked a rumor that I was attempting to sleep with "Dayna's man." It wasn't even serious between me and Max in the first place. I did like him, though I didn't see it going anywhere. I chalked our night together up to a drunk weekend in Palm Springs, as I wasn't interested in being with him again. We were friends who still flirted and nothing more.

After Palm Springs, Max and Dayna decided that they were going to give their relationship a real shot, which I was totally fine with. I was happily single, traveling to Vegas to meet friends when we had time off on Sundays and Mondays. Since we were filming five days a week, we weren't seeing each other much outside of work, and it felt like everyone on the show was moving in different directions, especially since I didn't fit in as the single one.

One day a few weeks after the trip, production thought it would be a good idea for me to have a conversation with Dayna in the back alley of SUR, so she could confront me about being jealous of her and Max. This turned out to be the infamous scene where I was using my inhaler, because I was having a panic attack, and when I broke the fourth wall by screaming at Jeremiah. I was at my breaking point. I felt like I'd done nothing but lived my life for the show for years and they were taking advantage of my goodwill, time after time, season after season. I'd had enough.

I explained to Dayna, in no uncertain terms, that my issue was not with her and Max. It was that I'd been demoted and had my pay reduced. Also, that I'd built my career outside of the show for the last two and a half years and that they never featured any of it—while she'd just walked into SUR and they were highlighting her stand-up comedy shows, which every cast member was invited to attend, except me.

Miraculously, in that moment, she acknowledged what I was saying. And it was gratifying that she finally knew why I'd been frustrated all season. I was still making a lot more money than she was on the show, but I'd been paving the way for seven years prior so that new girls like Dayna could come work at SUR and have their opportunity to shine. For the first time since the demotion, I felt like someone really understood my feelings about the whole situation.

Dayna and I became friends right after that and even ended up going to my house in Palm Springs for the Fourth of July. It was on that off-camera trip where we completely bonded, staying up and talking until the sun came up and getting to know each other far beyond the Max of it all. It felt rewarding that we could carve out a friendship when it felt like production had been pitting the two of us against each other. We're still friends to this day. Conversely, things did not work out with her and Max, which I could have told her would happen from the beginning.

Through all of the season eight drama, I was also freezing my eggs. This made filming and all of that season's drama even more challenging for me, both because it was such an emotional process and because I was sober for some of it to prep my body. I was single and shooting myself up with hormones alone, my future uncertain in more ways than one. The show touched on it briefly, but it definitely wasn't taken seriously. It was actually my second go at freezing my eggs. My first round had been in January 2019, though I'd only come away with a few mature eggs. My doctor recommended that I do it again so that they could extract enough eggs to really feel secure. As the eggs go through the thawing and fertilization process, many of them don't survive. Then, once you genetically test them, you can lose even more.

Unfortunately, none of my cast members were in similar positions, so they didn't understand what I was going through. I was mildly depressed, sober, and freezing my eggs for a family that I might or might not have, while they were all in happy relationships and more secure at work. It felt like I didn't have any support.

When the season finally aired and I watched it back, I was very surprised by how the show was edited. There was this new guy, Brett Caprioni, whom I'd met right before we started filming, because Lisa was using him as a personal trainer. She'd asked me to show him the ropes, and I was totally game because he was hot. So, we hung out one night in Santa Monica, got a few drinks, went back to my house, played some games, and had a very short make-out session around 5 a.m.

The next day before filming, we were working at SUR together, and I said, "I'm not going into this season hooking up with a new guy at SUR. I had the whole Adam thing last season. And it's not going to be a good look for me, so let's just pretend like that never happened."

He agreed and we told everyone we were just new friends who grabbed drinks with a group on the west side. But then as Brett was asking Max about me, Max told him that I was "boy crazy"—on the same night I'd first met Dayna—which really pissed me off when I saw it on-screen. Needless to say, that was not a fun night for me, and I really didn't appreciate the new guys talking about me behind my back. Was I attracted to Brett? Sure, we had kissed. But that was it. When the show aired it looked like I was pining for Brett and totally obsessed with him, and that he was so grossed out by me, which was not the case at all. I had genuinely learned my lesson the season prior when I slept with Adam and ruined the friendship. I was not about to go for round two with Brett. This was especially frustrating given that I'd put those guardrails up—not to date another server at SUR—and because of how I felt like the odd girl out with the other couples.

When it did actually come out that Brett and I had kissed toward the end of filming, production was furious with me that they didn't have that information earlier on. They said it could have been on the show and that I was hiding parts of my life from them. I replied, "You don't pay me enough to get the full story. I hid it because I was worried how it was going to make me look, which you're now doing anyway." They had proven me totally right.

One of the editors, Bri Dellinger, actually ended up going

on a podcast after the season wrapped and said that her favorite thing to do while working on the show was to find my most cringeworthy moments and piece them together. How gross is that? I never spoke about it because I was a team player, but that didn't make it any less hurtful. Honestly, it seemed like it was totally unearned animosity, and like I was being targeted for no reason. It would've been easy for the editors to make any cast member look silly, as it would be for any person if their daily life was being filmed, but I was singled out. After appearing on the podcast, Bri was fired.

I mean how could someone purposely sit at their desk and think: What else can I do today to make Scheana look even more cringe? It reawakened my trauma from being bullied in middle school and by the mean girls at SUR. Only this time was different, because it wasn't coming from my peers, it was from someone I'd entrusted with my authentic story and my vulnerability.

It's a shame that there are people like that in this industry and world who see us as "characters" on a TV show and not actually human.

There was a particular scene with Brett that was a perfect example of these editorial hijinks. We were on the front patio at SUR, and the editors spliced together two separate parts of our conversation to make me look bad. People online even noticed how the light kept changing, since we filmed around sunset. The first part of the conversation was about how I knew his ex-girlfriend, who was a really big YouTuber. I was saying how he was such a catch and what a bummer it was that it didn't work out with them because he seemed like a great guy, and any girl would be lucky to have him. I also said that he and I were just friends and never going to be more. He agreed. But when the final episode aired, it seemed like I was telling him he was this amazing catch and he was letting me down by not dating me. It was completely ridiculous and off base.

That same season, when Stassi and Beau got engaged, some of the cast was sitting at the table at Lisa Vanderpump's house, and they put me next to Stassi's fifteen-year-old brother, Nikolai, whom I'd known since he was in kindergarten. The producers told me that they wanted to feature Nikolai in the scene more, so they prompted me to ask him about school, sports, whether he had a girlfriend now that he was older, etc. I was teasing him, as I would a younger brother, thinking nothing of it. That is, until the final episode made it look like I was hitting on Nikolai. I was *shocked*; he was *fifteen*.

But, as usual, I was able to move past it for a few reasons. For one, there were enough good moments from the season to keep me going—scenes that I felt truly captured my experience or gave viewers a look at the real me and the things I was struggling with at the time. Also, I still felt lucky to work with so many friends and to be able to share my story publicly, which I knew people would relate to. Plus, we had a lot of fun times and trips. And the steady paycheck certainly made it worthwhile. I wasn't ready for any of that to end.

Thankfully, when season nine rolled around, my demotion was lifted. I thought I had proven myself and was finally in the clear.

Little did I know it would happen a second time, for season ten.

10

LIAR LIAR

Looking back, my first marriage was doomed to fail because it was built on a foundation of lies. Like most addicts, Shay was dishonest about many things, but I was dishonest, too. I denied his problem to my friends and my family by insisting that our relationship was secure and by pretending that his addiction was the only issue in our marriage. But for months I was scared and lonely, with no one to talk to about what was really going on, until finally I had no choice but to face the truth.

So maybe it should have felt concerning when my relationship with my current husband, Brock Davies, began with a series of three lies. Now, hear me out—they were all *good* lies. Yes, there is such a thing!

Let's rewind for a minute to when we were filming season eight. As I mentioned, I felt like I didn't really fit in with all the couples. On top of that, I just wasn't in a good place. While I wasn't necessarily looking for a serious relationship, my strategy of dating random guys who meant nothing to me wasn't working out, either. Some were losers who were fun to look at and had chiseled abs, some were retired athletes with baby mamas (but not wives or girlfriends), and some were just unemployed. What they had in common was how uninterested I was in all of them. At the time, I didn't feel like taking care of anyone but myself.

As I said, I was freezing my eggs, single, sad, and hormonal, thinking about—at some point—potentially having a baby by myself. It didn't actually occur to me that maybe one day my future husband and I would need to do IVF with those eggs. Instead, my concern was that I didn't want to wake up at forty, alone and without the option of carrying my own child.

In the midst of seeing all these random guys, I met someone. That April, while I was at Stagecoach, there was this girl, DD, at Neon Carnival. She was about five nine, with dark hair, brown eyes, and tattoos, and she was drop dead gorgeous. We'd each had an awkward run-in with our respective exes—mine being Rob and his new girlfriend—that weekend, which was crushing, and we bonded over that instantly. Since we had mutual friends, we didn't feel like complete strangers.

DD and I were both having terrible nights because our friends had left us to hang out with other guys, so we went to an after-party and talked until 5 a.m. The following day, we met up at the festival, and it felt like we'd known each other for years. We just had this instant connection and mutual love for Sam Hunt. I was newly into the country scene, and he was one of the first artists I really gravitated toward.

When we got back to LA, we started hanging out all the time and became almost inseparable. It was beginning to feel like we were closer than just friends. One night, we went to dinner, just the two of us, to Craig's in West Hollywood and walked in holding hands. We didn't care if the paparazzi snapped pictures, we were happy to be seen together. After that, when we were at TomTom for the evening, she kissed me out of nowhere, which I wasn't expecting but really enjoyed. From there, for the next couple of months, it became this thing where we would get drunk, make out, and tell people we were dating. It never went beyond that; we were just friends who drunkenly made out often. We were both talking to guys, too, but they were all fuck boys. I was definitely attracted to her, though I also didn't give it much thought in the beginning, because I didn't think I was going to get into a serious relationship with a woman.

One weekend in September 2019, DD and I and two of our other friends decided to go down to San Diego for the KAA-BOO music festival, which was where I had reconnected with Rob a few years earlier. After night two of the festival, we went to a nightclub called Oxford Social Club, where a promoter invited us to sit at his table with some of his friends. Initially, I was wary because I'd once been drugged at a promoter table at Les Deux in Hollywood, but since this guy was a friend of a friend, I felt pretty safe.

DD and I danced for hours, chatted up this table of new friends, and didn't want the night to end. So, when the promoter invited us to an after-party, we were totally game. The after-party was supposed to be at a guy named Brock's apartment until it got relocated to another house. We hadn't met Brock yet as he wasn't at the club with us, but when we got to the after-party, he initially hit on DD. It wasn't at all surprising that a guy would hit on her, as she was so beautiful, and he and I hadn't even seen each other yet. Though, after they'd been talking for a few, he realized that she had that typical "hot girl who knows she's hot" attitude and the best resting bitch face, which he wasn't into. Their personalities just didn't click.

There were only about fifteen people at the house, so, eventually, our paths crossed. Brock had long hair at the time, which totally reminded me of Jason Momoa. I thought, Wow, this guy looks like Aquaman. He was hot, even though he dressed a little funny, in loafers with tight pants that stopped at his ankles. He definitely didn't look like he was from LA, but he had a certain swagger that attracted me to him.

I detected his accent immediately, which I thought was so sexy, and asked if he was from Australia or New Zealand. He said he'd lived both places, which was cool, because I'd just been to Auckland and Sydney with my friends Janet and Courtney a few months earlier. I pulled up some photos on my phone to show him of me with koalas and jumping off the Sky Tower in Auckland, as if he cared—but he acted like he did.

When the party was over, I called an Uber to take us back to our hotel, and Brock offered to walk us outside, which was very gentlemanly. It was pretty chilly, so he was hugging me while we waited for the car to come. He even opened the car door for me, once it arrived. But he didn't ask for my number or Instagram. I was a little surprised, since we'd had such a nice conversation, but honestly I figured I'd never see him again.

The next morning, one of my friends told me that Oxford Social Club had posted a video on Instagram and to check my

DMs. I saw that it was a cute Boomerang of me and the girls, and—directly beneath it—was a DM from an account called @b.the.lion. I opened it, and it was a message from Brock saying, *Hey, nice meeting you last night. If you like football, the next time I'm in LA, I'd love to take you to a Rams game.* I looked at my profile, and the last photo I'd posted was of me at a Chargers game, so that must have given him the idea. I appreciated that he noticed and led with that, rather than just asking me out for a drink, which is much more cliché. I responded, saying, *I'm in, as long as there's an away Chargers game that day.* I have season tickets to the Chargers, and I wasn't going to miss a home Chargers game to go watch the Rams. He then asked if I was still in San Diego, and I told him that we were there and planning to go to the festival again that day.

Brock said he was going as well, which I'd later learn was lie number one, because he didn't actually have a ticket. He just wanted an excuse to see me. Even though I wasn't aware of this, I let him know that I had two extra VIP wristbands that he and a friend could have if they wanted. He thanked me and said he'd pick them up at my hotel whenever we were ready.

After I was dressed, I went down to the hotel bar to meet him. Almost immediately, Brock shared with me that he had two kids back in Australia and an ex-wife. I thought his honesty was refreshing, but I was also like, Okay, bro, I just met you last night. I don't need your whole life story. I'm just here to give you some wristbands to the music festival. He then showed me photos of his daughter and son, which was sweet, though I still didn't think I was going to see him past that day.

Regardless, I was excited to have fun with my friends and

for Brock to join us. While we were at the festival together, somehow the movie *Dirty Dancing* came up and Brock said, "I can do that lift into the air like the guy does in the movie." And a friend of mine said, "No, you can't. Prove it." Brock was up for the challenge and instructed me to run to him, so he could hoist me over his head. I liked his confidence, so I did it. As I was coming down, he kissed me for the first time, and I thought: Uh-oh, trouble. I liked it, and definitely felt something. After that, we hung out for the rest of the night. He even put me on his shoulders while we were leaving the final set. Still, to me, it just seemed like a fun little fling in San Diego.

From there, we ended up at a bar in Pacific Beach with Max Boyens, who Brock also knew from San Diego. They put on my song, "Good As Gold," and I got up on the bar. (Shocking, I know.) I was pouring shots down people's throats and ignoring Brock. One of my friends came up to me and said, "Brock looks like a sad puppy over there in the corner. You should go hang out with him." I was there to hang out with my friends, but I felt bad, so I went over to talk with him for a bit. The more we chatted, the more I was intrigued. He wasn't like any of the guys I knew in LA or anyone I'd ever met before. Maybe it was the fact that he wasn't from the United States. Either way, I wanted to see him more.

At the end of the night, we exchanged numbers and—from then on—we were in touch every day, just chatting and sharing details from our days. I was developing a serious crush on him. Two weeks later, a couple of friends and I went to another festival in San Diego called CRSSD, which Brock got us tickets to. He also arranged for a very nice Airbnb for us to stay in. We had so much fun at the festival and stayed out until 5 a.m. with Max and another friend. Brock ended up sleeping over, since he had a roommate at the time. Nothing happened between us until the following morning when my friends went to brunch and left us alone in the Airbnb. That was when we had the most incredible sex I'd ever had in my life, and I was hooked.

I remember being in bed with Brock and realizing that I was holding his hand incorrectly with my ring and my pinky fingers touching. While I was wondering if he noticed, he was insecure that I'd noticed that on his left hand, his pointer finger was gone and the top of his middle finger down to his knuckle was also missing. Oddly, I had no clue. I thought I was the awkward one. And he didn't say a word about it.

Later that evening, when it was time for me to return to LA, I was feeling really sick, so Brock offered to drive me home and then take the train back to San Diego, which was very sweet. While we were in the car, we were holding hands again. Clearly feeling like he had to call it out, he said, "I need to tell you something." He ungripped his hand from mine, held it up, and said, "Crocodile, four years old." I was totally caught off guard and also didn't know that this was lie number two.

That night Brock cooked me the most amazing dinner—spaghetti with vegetables and chicken served with fresh ginger tea for my cold—which endeared him to me even more. Sadly, the following day, he had to go back to San Diego. I had the main titles shoot for the opening credits of season eight for *Vanderpump Rules*, and I remember telling Katie about how great Brock was, even though I obviously wasn't fully committed to him yet. I thought we really had a chance at something special, so the distance didn't bother me at all. I loved San Diego and could imagine visiting him there more, or going back and forth.

One week after I slept with Brock, I went with DD and a couple of other friends to Las Vegas for the same RiSE Lantern Festival I'd been at the previous year. It was her birthday, so we were going to celebrate.

After the festival in San Diego, DD realized she'd left her favorite jacket behind. Brock was supposed to send it with his friend who was driving to Vegas, but he forgot. And DD really wanted to wear it to her birthday dinner. So, Brock, being a gentleman, got on an airplane and flew to Vegas to bring it to her. He said he didn't want her to feel disappointed on her birthday, and he also wanted to do it for me. I thought he really went above and beyond, but I told him that I was on a girls' trip and that I was with DD that weekend. Yes, I'd slept with Brock the week prior, but he wasn't my boyfriend, and even though I had feelings for him, I also still really liked DD and didn't want to ditch her, especially for a guy, on her special weekend. Thankfully, Brock understood.

When I told my friends what he'd done, they surprisingly said it was cool if he came out with us, especially because Brock had just done DD a huge favor. I was kind of annoyed because I was there to be with DD, and I knew we were going to be making out, but I figured it was his prerogative if he wanted to stay and bear witness to that, which he did.

I think maybe DD saw his presence as a challenge or a reason to show off. Most men like watching two girls make out, so we did exactly that. I'd go and dance on him and then go back and make out with her. I loved not feeling constrained at all, not being committed to either one of them.

Everyone else was having a good time, too, especially because I did everything I could to make DD's birthday perfect.

I arranged for bottle service, took care of dinner, and I remained pretty sober in order to stay in control of every detail. I also gave DD plenty of attention, so she didn't feel jealous of Brock.

The truth is, she brought guys around, too. (One was an Olympic snowboarder with a gold medal.) We always supported each other dating other people, in part because we also had our time together. I think we were both afraid to take it further or actually have "the talk" about really dating each other. Part of me was worried about what some of my extended conservative relatives would think, even though my immediate family is very liberal. I was also concerned with what the *VPR* audience would think. Everything I did was judged and somehow wrong, so I was afraid people would think my feelings for DD were fake and that I was doing it for attention or to follow a trend. (Miley Cyrus had recently started dating a woman.)

The whole thing was very confusing, so a million questions would run through my mind when I tried to unpack our relationship. Was I bisexual? Was I just attracted to her? I had been into other women in the past, but I'd never had the level of feelings I had for DD, and I didn't understand why. Also, in the past with other women, there was always a man involved, if you know what I'm saying. Was I just lonely and over men? Had I simply met her at the right place and time? I mean, I'd just run into Rob and his girlfriend, whom he'd started dating after me. Maybe it was a reaction to that? Whatever it was, it felt like more than friendship but not enough to admit or commit to a relationship. Part of me wishes I'd expressed to DD how I was feeling, to see if she felt the same, but the fear of rejection outweighed finding out what we could be for me.

In the midst of the birthday insanity and trying to sort out my feelings, I completely forgot that it was October 2, which was the day Collin passed away.

When we got back to the hotel, we were all getting in the elevator, and suddenly Brock said, "Wait, I've got to run to the gift shop and grab some water." At that point, I was so exhausted that I didn't want to delay getting into bed. I was happy to drink the overpriced Fiji water in the room. But he insisted, and we held the elevator for him. Before I knew what was happening, Brock came running back with a bottle of Jameson. He said, "I noticed you didn't take a shot for your friend all night, and I know how important that is to you." I couldn't believe he'd remembered that. I had tears in my eyes, and all of my friends, including DD, were like, Scheana, accept it, embrace it. But I didn't want to admit that I was falling for Brock, because I felt like I was just getting comfortable exploring things with a woman, and I knew getting serious with him would mean closing myself off to some extent. Still, we all did shots, Brock slept in a chair in our hotel room that night, and then he went home to San Diego early the next morning.

After that, we started hanging out regularly, traveling back and forth between LA and San Diego. He then told me that he was going to Australia for six weeks, to play in a rugby game and visit his family. He asked if I wanted to join him for part of the trip, which sounded super fun. We'd just wrapped season eight, I had all the time in the world, and I didn't want to be without him for that long, so I agreed to meet him there.

The first two or three weeks while he was away, we talked on the phone every single day and FaceTimed. He also went to Bali with friends, and I was totally jealous, which I made known. I couldn't wait to get there, too, and experience everything with him. I had a major crush, and I wasn't sleeping with anyone else. Brock actually met my parents in person before he left for the airport, and my mom said she liked his style. I laughed, because that was the one thing I thought he needed to change!

I was basically giddy my entire long flight to meet up with him. When Brock met me at Brisbane Airport it was like a scene out of a movie. He was standing there waiting for me, lifted me up in the air, and gave me the most electric kiss of my life. I felt it all the way down to my toes. Full body tingles. I'd never felt that way about anyone. It was more than butterflies.

On one of our many phone calls, I'd told Brock how much I loved koalas and that I wanted to hug one. When I'd been at the Sydney Zoo earlier that year, I was only able to get close but not touch. So when he immediately drove me to Currumbin Wild-life Sanctuary to hug a koala, it was a major swoon. Between the Jameson and the koala, I appreciated that Brock not only truly listened to what I said but also delivered.

Our day at the sanctuary was incredible. They have a wild-life conservation center and a wildlife hospital, as Australia has hundreds of critically endangered species and this sanctuary helps save them. They do a lot of rehabilitation for koalas and kangaroos there, which we heard about from the staff and then saw a bit of ourselves. It was incredible to witness, and it made me feel hopeful about the future of these species and the lives of the individual animals. Brock actually "adopted" a koala for me! I laughed so hard about that, because I'd once adopted a pen-guin for Adam, which they covered on *VPR*. Of course Brock didn't know that, and he felt a little silly once I told him, but I assured him that it was really sweet.

After hugging the koalas and snapping photos, one of the

sanctuary's employees recommended that we head straight to the crocodile exhibit, to which I said, "No thanks." "What else do you suggest?" Brock asked, "Do you not like crocodiles?" It was a bit awkward, as the sanctuary employee stood there awaiting my answer, but I was trying to be subtle. I then motioned to Brock's hand, so he'd understand my concern. I thought the crocodiles might be triggering for him, though when he didn't pick up on my reluctance, I finally mentioned it.

This was when I found out that Brock had lied about his hand. He smirked and said, "Oh my God, I was joking." I said, "Wait, what? I told all of my friends and production that you'd wrestled a crocodile at four years old. You're now telling me, six weeks in, that it was a lie!?" He nodded and explained the truth, which was that his hand got caught and crushed in the gears of an electric gate on his family's farm. To make matters worse, since where he lived was so rural, he had to go to a veterinarian to have it bandaged up before being airlifted to the nearest hospital. I can't even imagine how traumatizing that must have been. (Our daughter, Summer, is now around the age that it happened to him!)

Even though I'd totally believed him, I couldn't be upset that Brock had lied, as he also said that he'd been bullied by kids at school for not having all of his fingers, so his mom told him to tell them he'd fought off a croc in order to sound tough. I thought that was funny and endearing, and I really felt for him because I understood what it was like to be bullied at such a young age.

After our sanctuary visit, Brock wanted me to meet his mom and sister. We went out to dinner with them that night, and I really felt like I was becoming part of his inner circle. I would have loved to meet Brock's children, but it was early in our relationship, and that wasn't even an option at the time. I also knew his kids were being raised by their stepdad, similar to the way I was raised by my stepfather. I think having this parental framework helped me to understand the complexities of Brock's situation with his kids. They have a stepdad who is a consistent father figure in their lives, and just like Raul had given my parents space to create a family unit, it appeared that Brock had done the same. Now, I'm not saying this is right or wrong, nor the appropriate thing to do, but I understood it. Meeting his mom and sister was more than enough for me to get a better peek into Brock's world, and I was ready to move on to the next leg of our trip.

The following day, we were scheduled to go to Uluru, which is a massive sandstone monolith in the heart of the Northern Territory's Red Centre. I'd known about it for weeks and was very excited to see what he'd described as a cool light field that looked like the northern lights, but on the ground. I'd even brought my Timberland boots for our outback adventure.

At the airport, Brock took care of everything, which I thought was very chivalrous. I had no idea that he had an ulterior motive or that everyone we interacted with was in on another "lie." However, I did notice that none of the gates said Uluru.

The amusing thing was that, when we got to our gate, the flight attendant recognized me from *VPR*. Unbeknownst to me, Brock thought he was screwed and was praying that she'd stick to the script and not fuck things up for him. Fortunately, she played her part perfectly, and I was none the wiser. Once we were on the jetway, I decided to take a video with Brock, where I was talking about how pumped I was to visit Uluru. Meanwhile, all of the other passengers were looking at me like I was crazy. I'm used to catching stares from strangers, so I didn't think twice about it.

Finally, we boarded the plane, and Brock had a whole plan to get my noise-canceling headphones on me before the captain made his announcements. But just as we were settling into our seats, another passenger was trying to shove his bag into the overhead compartment and it wouldn't fit. The flight attendant told him he had to check his bag, but he didn't want to. After a quick back-and-forth, she finally said, "Sir, when we land in Bali, you'll get your luggage. We have to check it now."

I guess I was completely naïve—and definitely not good with geography—because I was wondering, Do we have a lay-over in Bali on our way to Uluru? I didn't have much of a chance to think it through, as the pilot then came over the loudspeaker and said, "We have a five-and-a-half-hour flight to Denpasar." He didn't mention anything about connecting to Uluru after touching down in Bali's capital city.

I started looking around the plane and noticed that no one else was dressed for the middle of the Outback. I motioned to my Timberlands and asked Brock, "Are we going to Bali?" He smiled and said, "Surprise!" I couldn't believe he'd kept the secret (lie number three) for that long. Even though I was kept in the dark, he'd been texting with my mom the entire time, so she had a full itinerary of our plan, as she can be a worrier.

We spent a couple of nights in Ubud, in the jungle, went to the Monkey Forest, took ATVs through the mud and waterfalls, got massages, and had some of the most delicious dinners I've ever experienced. Then we stayed in this massive Airbnb on a black sand beach in Canggu, a resort village on the south coast of Bali, and it was incredible. It was a six-bedroom house with a chef, a masseuse, and someone who did hair masks, scalp massages, and braids. The best part was that it was only $200 in U.S. currency a night for all of that. Everything was so affordable. Even when we went to a club in Seminyak for bottle service, they had two-for-one bottles. We couldn't even finish one, so we were passing around vodka to the other clubgoers.

That night at the club, Brock told me he loved me for the first time. While our relationship was still young, it felt right. It was the most amazing trip, and I was fully in love, too. Of course, that was terrifying to me, because—in my experience to that point—things that seemed too good to be true usually were.

When we returned from Bali, all my friends wanted to meet Brock, so we planned a night out in Venice at a bar called Roosterfish. Fifteen of my friends came, including DD. I remember when she walked in that night, she was so excited to see me but I could see it in her eyes that she could tell that I was crazy about Brock and that I was pulling away from her.

A few weeks later, she and I were out in LA drinking a lot and, just like old times, she kissed me. Brock was there as well, and he lost his cool. He stormed out of the bar, I followed him, and he said, "You're my girlfriend now. You don't do that shit. You guys had a thing and that ends now or I'm gone." Clearly, he was not the kind of guy who was down with his woman drunkenly making out with a woman she'd had a relationship with.

So I knew that I had to put my foot down with DD. I told her that we couldn't make out anymore, because I didn't want

Brock to be upset or to break up with me, and then I started distancing myself from her to protect my new relationship.

Ultimately, DD ended up sending me a long text saying that she understood that Brock and I were exclusive but that we'd been such close friends, and I'd just discarded her without consideration for her feelings. I felt so badly that I'd hurt her, and I was hurt to lose her as well. Still, I knew that if I was going to be with Brock I couldn't have someone in my life whom I was still attracted to. We tried to stay friends for about six months but grew apart as we began talking less and less. As painful as losing DD was for me, I knew I was making the right choice.

Brock was my person; he still is. Actually one of the many things that convinced me of this was when I brought him to BravoCon in 2019. Unlike Rob, Brock was super comfortable with the reality TV stuff. He didn't try to be the center of attention, and he was so nice to every fan who came up to us, which was opposite of some of the other boyfriends. Brock couldn't understand why they'd act that way. His feeling was that, without fans, there would be no *VPR*, and he knew how important the show was to me. He was happy to take photos with anyone who asked, even though he said no one knew who he was.

Brock also helped me feel more comfortable with the other couples on the show, because he fit seamlessly into those relationships and my life, despite the fact that—given my track record with men—my castmates were very protective of me and wary about him, as they were with any new person who came into the mix.

I thought, If this guy can handle this type of scrutiny and attention so gracefully, he really might be the one.

11

KNOCKED UP

Before I met Brock, I was never the type of woman who just *had* to be a mom. I went back and forth for years on whether or not I wanted kids, which depended on my career and relationship status during those times. When I was single Scheana in my early twenties, I couldn't imagine ever wanting children. Then I got married, and I could really picture Shay as a great dad someday and was excited to start a family with him. Obviously, that didn't work out.

I'm sure some of my wishy-washiness came from not knowing if I could even get pregnant. I started birth control at age twelve because my period was so irregular, and I always had this weird gut feeling that it wouldn't be easy for me to conceive. Fast-forward through a divorce to being single at thirty-three with no potential baby daddies in the picture; I decided it was time to get my fertility tested. At least then I would know where I stood.

As it happened, that weird gut feeling I had was right: Getting pregnant would be extremely difficult for me. My doctor said that my AMH levels—the hormone that determines egg count—should have been between 1.4 and 4.2. I was at 0.26. Severely low. As usual, I was Scheana the perfectionist, wanting to understand how to get that number up. Unfortunately, that was impossible. Those levels only go down as time goes on, and there's nothing you can do to raise them. That was really hard news to hear. Even if I wasn't 100 percent sure that I wanted to be a mom, I wasn't ready to rule it out, either. It felt unfair that the decision was seemingly being made for me.

My fertility doctor cut straight to the chase. He said that by the time I was in a relationship and ready to have a kid, it would be highly unlikely that I'd be able to get pregnant naturally. The best thing I could do was to freeze my eggs, but my biological clock was ticking really fast, so we had to start as soon as possible. They put me on a ton of supplements, and I started prepping my body immediately, which was a lot to process. I was sober for fifty-plus days—no alcohol or weed—straight through the holidays. I wasn't necessarily ready for that level of detox, as it meant no espresso martinis on Christmas and no champagne toast on New Year's Eve, but it didn't matter. I knew I needed to preserve my chance of ever being a mom.

After my next cycle, I did hormone injections for about two weeks, and when I went in for the egg-retrieval process, we got twelve eggs, only nine of which were mature enough. This was on the lower end of normal, so my doctor recommended I do a second round.

There were two big differences between my first and second rounds of freezing my eggs. Number one was the side effects. If you've frozen your eggs, you probably know that all the hormones and prenatals can have some interesting side effects. I didn't experience any of them during my first round, but the second time was a whole different story. The doctor put me on new supplements that made me nauseous, and my hormone injections made me…well, hormonal. As I mentioned, this was a bigger deal because I was also filming season eight of *Vanderpump Rules* at the time. I ended up coming across as super dramatic. It's true that I was extremely emotional, just not for the reasons most people thought.

With two rounds of egg freezing—and sixteen eggs banked—I felt satisfied with my results. And in September of that same year, I met Brock, which was roughly six months before the pandemic. Like most couples, we went into isolation together and got to know each other much faster than we would have if life had played out normally. Even though Brock and I hadn't been together very long, we both already knew that we were a done deal, and I also knew that I wanted to build a family with him one day. Still, I was in no rush to get pregnant, so we talked about the possibility of freezing embryos. I had already decided to do a third round of egg freezing in June 2020 with Ariana, but this time I figured, since I already had sixteen eggs, maybe we should make straight embryos. It was her first round and, as I'd done it twice before, we thought it would be nice to have each other's support if we went through it together.

Right before I started the process of getting my body ready again, Brock and I went on a trip to Lake Havasu in Arizona, and while we were there, I got really sick from just three drinks.

I assumed it was because I'd mixed hard liquor and wine or because I hadn't had anything to drink for a few weeks. Whatever the reason, I didn't think too much of it.

After the trip, I went back to Palm Springs with a friend, while Brock went to San Diego for work. I had a psychic reading scheduled, which was something I did on occasion, and I always asked my psychic about the same two things: future babies and future love interests. During this particular reading, my psychic said something weird and ambiguous—that if I wanted a baby, there was a child waiting for me that very day. I thought that she was referring to my frozen eggs.

However, when I got off the call, I realized that I was supposed to get my period a few days earlier. And that those three drinks had made me really sick in Lake Havasu. But my doctor had said it would be close to impossible for me to get pregnant, so I reasoned that I was just overthinking.

Still…I needed to know for sure.

My friend graciously made the run to CVS so I didn't have to risk getting recognized while buying pregnancy tests, and I sat with Brock on FaceTime while I peed on the stick. I was acting pretty casual about the whole thing, which Brock thought was funny. At that point, I had probably taken about twenty pregnancy tests in my lifetime, and none of them were positive. Why would this one be any different? But when I checked the test, as it turned out, "close to impossible" did not mean "impossible." The results were conclusive: I was pregnant.

It had to be a fluke. Not only was I freaking out, but I was totally in denial. My friend ran back to CVS and got a few more tests from different brands, including the digital ones that aren't just potential faint lines. One clearly said PREGNANT. I was shocked but also excited. I'd defied the odds. I was going to be a mom. If Brock was internally freaking out, he never showed it.

Of course, I had to get blood work done to actually confirm it, so I called my fertility doctor, the one who told me it was close to impossible that I would ever get pregnant naturally, and I said something to the effect of "What the fuck?!" They weren't supposed to be taking appointments for anyone less than ten weeks pregnant, but given how improbable this pregnancy was, he let me come in early to give me peace of mind.

I walked into that doctor's office with my vlog camera on, ready to capture everything. Due to the COVID pandemic, I wasn't allowed to bring Brock with me, so I wanted to record every second of the appointment to show him later. Brock and I had also just started our YouTube channel that February right before the world shut down, and in this weird, isolating time, I was really grateful and excited to share my fertility journey with my community online. As we were doing the ultrasound, my doctor told me to turn my camera off, and I figured it was a privacy thing, so I did. But then he explained he had something to say that I probably didn't want to record. It wasn't good news.

Yes, I was technically pregnant, but based on my last period, I should've been at about five and a half weeks. At that point, there should have already been a yolk sac, but there wasn't. He told me that he didn't think the pregnancy would progress. I don't remember exactly how I responded, but I know what I wanted to say was "fuck you." This man had told me I likely couldn't get pregnant at all, and there I was, pregnant. Why should I believe him that it wouldn't work out? I was determined to prove him wrong and carry this miracle baby to term.

As much as I didn't want to have faith in him, I agreed to

schedule an appointment with my ob-gyn, Dr. Banooni, the following week for another ultrasound and blood work to see how the pregnancy was progressing. In the meantime, Brock had a birthday to celebrate. We went out to dinner with a few of his friends, and when we got home, I went to the bathroom and noticed that I had started spotting. My heart sank to the bottom of my stomach, but I googled it and saw it was relatively common to spot during the first trimester. This was normal, apparently, but I was scared.

The next day, I was still spotting. The day after that, there was even more blood. Not normal. Everything I was reading online looked like bad news, but I hung on to the tiniest sliver of hope that my baby was somehow going to be okay. When I went back in to see my ob-gyn, we did another ultrasound, and my worst nightmare came true; there wasn't a heartbeat. And, even though my HCG levels had risen, my progesterone was too low. He told me that the pregnancy was very unlikely to progress.

It felt like my entire world was crashing in on me. I remember looking at the ultrasound on the screen and seeing two little dark dots. I never knew how badly I wanted to be a mom until I got pregnant, and now I realized I wanted it more than anything. I'd even discussed baby names with my mom and great-aunt Shirley at lunch in Palm Springs and felt so enthusiastic about raising a child with Brock. Yes, the relationship was relatively new, and we were still in a pandemic, but it just felt right. It was my path. And it broke my heart to think that those dots were all I was ever going to see.

The doctor told me to take a week to try and let my body release the pregnancy naturally. While I was waiting, I was feeling particularly alone, without my boyfriend or good friends by my side. Brock was in San Diego, trying to get his gyms somewhat up and running again for outdoor workouts in the midst of the pandemic, and I was at my mom's house. I wanted to get back to my house in Palm Springs, because my cats were there and I wanted some time alone with Brock, who was supposed to meet me there. Yet, when I checked his location, I saw that he was on the golf course. I texted him to say that I thought he was coming home for dinner, to which he replied that he was playing golf, that he'd be there when he could. I guess it was his way of getting his mind off of the miscarriage, although I didn't appreciate feeling abandoned. I really needed someone to lean on that day, and this felt like something we should be riding out together.

In the meantime, Lala was also in Palm Springs with Randall, and she texted me to see if I needed anything. I asked her to come over, as I needed a friend and didn't want to be alone. She called and said that she couldn't visit immediately, but that she'd check on me in a little while, even though I was crying and screaming about Brock to her. When she did text me later, it was to ask if I wanted to join "all of them" for dinner. I didn't know who "all of them" were, and I wasn't really in the mood to be around other people besides those closest to me, so I said no. I later found out that it was Lala, Randall, Machine Gun Kelly, and Megan Fox. Why the hell would I want to go to dinner with two celebrities while I was actively miscarrying and crying my eyes out? I wanted Lala, whom I thought was my friend, to come comfort me.

Ultimately, I ended up sobbing in the shower, getting into bed, putting on a pregnancy-loss meditation, and crying myself to sleep, until Brock arrived with cold In-N-Out. Lala had said we could meet up the next day, but I was so upset that I don't even think I replied. Randall later group-texted us saying that they had to get their jet back to LA with Machine Gun Kelly and Megan Fox, so they wouldn't actually be able to hang out. I thought it was total bullshit that Lala would let him communicate something so frivolous while I was enduring such a profound loss. She finally texted at 10 p.m. that night and again four days later with a few very short words. I ignored both. It was too little, too late.

When the pregnancy didn't pass naturally, I had to schedule a D&C procedure to officially terminate it. The only person I wanted with me during the procedure was my mom. Since she'd experienced a miscarriage as well, her presence was very comforting to me. The doctors gave me some pills and, five excruciating minutes later, it was done. I miscarried my miracle baby. It was the worst pain I've ever felt, both physically and emotionally.

I kept thinking: Is this my fault? Could I have done something differently? I beat myself up agonizing about those three drinks I'd had in Lake Havasu, wondering if those had caused the miscarriage. Every doctor in the world could have told me that was impossible, but I still would have felt guilty. I think anyone who has miscarried would understand. When you're enduring that kind of unbelievable loss, it's easy to blame yourself, even if there's nothing you could have done.

Brock took such good care of me through my recovery. I had some painful cramping and bleeding, but physically, I mostly felt okay. Except I didn't want to feel okay. I wanted to be nauseous and tired. I wanted my boobs to hurt. I wanted to be pregnant. Brock and I were both mourning, and most days, he held me in his arms and just let me sob. As painful as it was, it was consoling to be in it with him, and to have him by my side.

There's no nice way of putting it. The whole thing was a mindfuck. I didn't think I could get pregnant, then all of a sudden I was, and then I blinked twice and it was all taken away.

Every week felt like a new highest high or lowest low, but after I finally got off the roller coaster, I experienced a new sense of certainty. I was freezing my eggs as a "just in case," but I had gone back and forth for years on whether or not I wanted kids. It took losing a pregnancy to know for sure. I wanted to be a mom, and I was going to do anything to make that happen.

My doctor explained that freezing my eggs had likely allowed for the pregnancy to happen in the first place. The hormones must have woken my body up. The D&C procedure would be a similar wake-up call for my body, so my best chance of getting pregnant and carrying a healthy baby to term would be to wait one more period and immediately try again. Dr. Banooni's professional medical advice? Get to it. To which I said…no chance. Brock and I knew that we wanted to have a baby together, but we were still in the middle of a pandemic. We weren't filming for *Vanderpump Rules*, my podcast had been dropped by PodcastOne, and Brock's gyms were closed, making our income a grand total of zero. We hadn't been together for very long, either, only about eight and a half months. It was a very stressful time. Even though I'd spoken to one of our producers and was confident the show would eventually return, Brock and I both agreed wholeheartedly that this was not the time to have a baby. I still had my eggs frozen, so we could revisit the topic down the road.

A few weeks passed, I had my next period, and Brock and I moved into our new house in San Diego, ready to start a fresh chapter in our lives. Maybe a little too ready. On our first day in our home, we woke up to the most beautiful morning with the breeze blowing in off the ocean…it was perfect. Obviously, we had to christen the place, and while we had both agreed we weren't going to try yet…I'll spare you the details, but let's just say Brock could work on his reflexes a bit. I remember looking at him with my jaw dropped and asking, "Did you just get me pregnant?!" He said there was no way…but the answer turned out to be yes.

For the next three weeks, I didn't smoke, I didn't drink, I didn't eat cheese…I know there are only certain cheeses you can't have while you're pregnant, but I gave them all up, just in case. We had a trip to Sedona around the corner for my sister's birthday, and we had some outdoorsy things planned that I was a teensy bit nervous about. Off-roading in a Jeep didn't sound very safe for a pregnant woman, but I still wasn't sure if I was pregnant. Right before we left for the trip, I took another test, and once again, two lines. It was positive.

My first reaction was excitement, but immediately after that, I felt nothing but pure fear. My doctor said this would be my most likely shot at a healthy pregnancy, but what if something happened again? Was I going to lose another baby? I couldn't handle a second miscarriage. I couldn't go through that devastation again. The intrusive thoughts I've since battled throughout raising Summer started the second I knew she existed. This was my one chance at a healthy pregnancy, and I was so worried about blowing it. I wasn't going to let anything harm my baby.

So what did I do? *Everything.* I did acupuncture. I did Reiki.

I continued working out, but I was extremely careful. Since we were still in the throes of a pandemic, Brock and I kept our circle very small, so we weren't putting me or the baby at risk. James and Raquel were two of the only friends we saw regularly because they were maintaining a tight circle, too, and they were willing to drive down to see us in San Diego or meet up with us in Palm Springs. Raquel and I got really close during those nine months, but I've since heard she said on her podcast that I had rules about who she could and couldn't be friends with at the time. That's a lie. This was late 2020 and early 2021, and I was cautious about who I was coming into contact with because I was terrified of jeopardizing my child's health and safety. I was beyond anxious for the entire first half of my pregnancy, and then, at twenty-two weeks and five days, I felt my baby for the first time. She was there. She was alive. The anxious thoughts didn't entirely go away, but it was an enormous sigh of relief to feel her and to know that this baby—our baby—was there with me.

From then on, I thrived through my pandemic pregnancy. Can you imagine a better time to be pregnant? There was nothing going on, so I never had to put on makeup or get dressed up, and we lived on the beach, so I was really enjoying my best life. Admittedly, I overdid it with the maternity photos, but I think I earned that right, didn't I? Based on what Dr. Banooni said, I felt like this could be my one and only chance at a healthy, natural pregnancy, so I was going to document absolutely every second. I shared as much of my journey as possible, and even with COVID isolating us, I felt this amazing sense of community online. So many women reached out to me about their own experiences with pregnancy after loss. We might have been keeping our circle small, but I never felt alone.

In April 2021, I went in for my thirty-nine-week appointment, which is the milestone where a lot of women are ready to get that kid out of them. That wasn't the case for me. I was fine with being pregnant, and at my appointment, I told my doctor I would be happy to go another two or three weeks to see if my baby came naturally…except for one little problem. We were just a couple weeks out from filming the next season of *Vanderpump Rules*. My doctor, Brock, and I all agreed that I needed time with my daughter before the cameras started following us. We gave it one more week, and when the baby didn't come naturally at forty weeks, I was induced the following day. It was just nine days before we started filming.

The first fifteen hours in the hospital went as planned. But, after my blood pressure spiked dangerously high, things took a big turn. The nurses informed me that I had preeclampsia and that I would need to be put on a magnesium drip immediately. They told me that this would make me feel extremely flu-like. I didn't believe them. That is, until I started to shake uncontrollably. Then the baby's heart rate plummeted, and I was freaking out. She was already so precious to me that I couldn't stand the thought of losing her. There I was, selfishly trying to have this baby so I could film a TV show, and her heart rate was dropping. I was rushing her out. I shouldn't have gotten induced. If my baby didn't make it, it would be all my fault.

Turns out, the exact opposite was true. It was a miracle that I was induced. Had I waited and given birth naturally, the doctors might not have caught my preeclampsia, and I could have had a stroke and died. Instead, they gave me painkillers and watched me and the baby like hawks. I was terrified, but Brock, my mom, and my sister, Cortney, stayed by my side for the following ten hours, and after forty minutes of pushing, I officially became a mom to the most perfect human being there ever was, Summer Moon.

Nothing about Summer's birth was what I had expected. In movies, babies cry the second they're born. My baby, on the other hand, was limp and blue, and she wasn't making a sound. I heard my mom say, "She's so beautiful," but I was panicking. The nurses were counting: forty seconds, forty-one seconds…why wasn't she crying? I felt like my heart was going to beat out of my chest. I had already been through a miscarriage. Had I given birth to a stillborn too? After about forty-five heart-pounding seconds, Summer finally cried for the first time. My baby. My daughter. That cry was the most stunning, soothing sound in the world.

It turns out this is really common with babies who are born while their mother is on a magnesium drip. They call them "mag babies," and they come out a little sleepy and blue. No one warned me of that, though, so I spent nearly a minute thinking I had lost another baby. It was the most frightening minute of my entire life followed by the most joy I've ever felt. I was officially a mom.

After the nurses cleaned her up a bit, they put my gorgeous, perfect daughter on my chest, and I got to enjoy motherhood for approximately one second. I just remember saying "We did it, Summer" and sobbing the happiest tears. Then the doctors sent my mom and sister out of the room. I needed to be transferred to the high-risk ICU because my preeclampsia was advancing to HELLP syndrome (hemolysis, elevated liver enzymes, low platelet count), which is an extremely rare condition with serious complications of high blood pressure during pregnancy and postpartum. It usually occurs before the thirty-seventh week of pregnancy but can also occur shortly after delivery. Many women are diagnosed with preeclampsia beforehand; however, I wasn't until fifteen hours into labor. We realized after that I'd had some signs at my forty-week appointment, but we chalked the high blood pressure up to nerves and thought the protein in my urine was a result of what I'd eaten for breakfast.

I was so confused and overwhelmed. I'd read up on everything during my pregnancy, but I'd somehow missed the chapter on HELLP syndrome. I had no idea what was happening with my body, but they took my baby away, and I was whisked off to the high-risk ICU. There, my doctor explained that my blood platelets were extremely low, and my liver enzymes were extremely elevated. What did that mean? I had to be put on blood pressure medication and stay on my magnesium drip for at least twenty-four hours. The catheter wasn't coming out anytime soon, either. I was completely lethargic but still shivering uncontrollably, like I had some terrible flu. I wasn't even allowed to hold Summer by myself without being monitored by a doctor or nurse.

I ended up spending five days in the hospital, and Brock never once left my side for anything other than grabbing a coffee or going to the bathroom. I don't even think he showered. When we finally brought Summer home, he and I had about three days to settle into our new lives as Mom and Dad. And those three days were filled with lactation consultants at our house, Zooms with sleep experts, my dad meeting Summer for the first time, endless diapers, pumping, and nursing. After that, boom! Cameras were up.

It was a shockingly jarring turnaround, but I don't think

the episodes really showed just how much whiplash there was. I practically crawled out of a bed in the ICU and into hair and makeup. The long conversations Brock and I had about me nearly dying ten days before filming didn't make the episode. Instead, the very first scene of season nine opened up with the two of us chatting about if Katie and Lala were coming to my hibachi birthday dinner. I had clearly been crying, but the hour we spent in the kitchen discussing the trauma I had just experienced was left on the cutting room floor. And, mind you, I was *still* in diapers.

Maybe *Vanderpump Rules* wasn't the right show to highlight my journey to motherhood. And, yes, Lala's intrauterine insemination (IUI) journey was a big part of season eleven of *VPR*, but back in seasons eight and nine, the show just wasn't there yet. It was frustrating that this enormous part of my life was cut, but that's how it goes with reality TV. I don't get to pick which parts of my life make it on air, but I do get to choose what I share off-screen. I barely survived childbirth, and whether or not that fits into an episode of *Vanderpump Rules*, it's a story that deserves to be told.

So many women have reached out to thank me for being so open about my miscarriage, my rainbow baby, and my traumatic labor. Some have told me about their own experiences with HELLP syndrome, and others have friends and sisters who weren't as lucky as I was. They didn't live to meet their own babies. I still get so many of these messages, and they break my heart, but they also remind me why I'm so open about these things. The more awareness I can bring to maternal health, the better.

Parenting in the spotlight is a really unique circumstance.

I'm lucky to have a whole group chat full of moms who get it. Now, after making up, Lala and I are practically raising our daughters as sisters, and the old petty drama just doesn't matter anymore. Moms have to stick together, especially the moms of the Bravo-verse.

When they say that being a parent changes you, they're really not kidding. I'll never be the same Scheana I was before I had Summer, and I don't want to be. I want to be the best version of myself as an example for my daughter. I've called Summer "Mini Scheana" since before she was born, and if this little girl really is a mini version of me, I'm intent on being strong, fierce, and forgiving. That's the kind of mother I want to be for her, and that's the kind of woman I want her to be someday.

12

MOTHER'S INSTINCT

In December 2021, less than a year after Summer was born, Andy Cohen asked whether Brock and I were planning on having another kid on the *Vanderpump Rules* season nine reunion. He wasn't the first and was far from the last person to ask me this, but it was still a difficult question for me to answer. After a miscarriage, a traumatic birth that nearly killed me, and some serious postpartum struggles that had yet to be diagnosed, carrying another baby sadly isn't in the cards for me. While Brock and I have discussed the possibility of a surrogate or an adoption, we also know that our family has already grown beyond the two of us and Summer.

To me, family has never been limited to just blood relatives, which goes all the way back to how I was raised. My dad may not be my biological father, but he's still my dad, full stop.

My mom and dad raised me as a team, and while my biological father was in the picture, he remained in the background. This taught me from the very beginning that family is built, not born, and families don't have to be traditional to be real and full of meaningful bonds.

They say it takes a village, and Brock and I chose to combine our village with Lala's, as we'd put all the bad blood behind us and were ready to join together in our parenting journeys. It started when we took a trip to San Diego for July 4, 2022, when Summer and Lala's daughter, Ocean, were a little over a year old. I didn't realize yet that I had postpartum OCD, and when I let an intrusive thought slip out—"What if Summer chokes?"— Lala had a calm, collected answer: "Well, then you do the back blows that they taught us in CPR class." It sounded so obvious, but I hadn't realized that my level of constant panic wasn't normal. Sure, as a new mom, Lala had her own fears, but they looked very different from mine and seemed much more rational to everyone, including me.

Over the course of the summer leading up to season ten, Lala and I became a lot closer, partly because she'd recently made the decision to leave Randall. Ocean was only seven months old, and Lala needed a solid friend and support system in her life. I really wanted to be that person for her, both because I loved her and because I could see how hard that experience was. I also genuinely wanted our girls to grow up together. I thought it would be so cool for them to have a best friend they would know their entire lives.

Even though our daughters were really bonding, as we were, I still never opened up to Lala about the deep-seated parental fears that had followed me since Summer's birth, and even my pregnancy, because I was afraid to say out loud how I actually felt. I just watched the way she mothered, and I admired how composed and collected she always seemed to be. I later learned that she, too, would freak out on occasion, but she had the ability to hold her shit together in a way that I couldn't. Not only did I respect this, but I envied it.

From there, Lala and I became a safe space for each other, and we started to combine our families even further. Our moms became friends, our friends became friends, and we even became closer with each other's siblings. We worked hard to create this big, extended family. Brock was also there for Lala, because at the time Ocean didn't have a solid father figure in her life aside from her uncle, Easton.

With the passing of time, both Lala and I understood what we needed and wanted from our friendship, and we did everything we could to nurture our connection. As mothers, we were the only cast members on the show who could fully understand each other. Unfortunately, Brittany and Stassi weren't part of the cast anymore, so even though they'd also just had babies, they weren't filming with us.

Still, as much of a help and inspiration as Lala was for me, I couldn't escape my own anxieties surrounding motherhood. Every minute of every day I was petrified that Summer might choke, fall down, stop breathing in her sleep, or get hit by a car. I agonized over every single thing, no matter how insignificant it seemed to other people. It was always something different and, no matter what it was, I'd play out an entire terrifying scenario in my head until I couldn't stop stressing about it. But I never wanted to tell anyone, because I thought they'd think I was crazy.

I'd taken all the baby CPR classes and read every precautionary tale in books and online, yet I remained panicked that I wouldn't know what to do if the worst actually happened. That was when Lala told me that Ocean had choked on a piece of cantaloupe and her mother's instinct had kicked in, she dislodged it, and Ocean was fine. There was no way I'd have been brave enough to give Summer a piece of food that could get lodged in her throat. What if she couldn't chew it? I would literally cut grapes into four tiny pieces. Practically everything she ate was pureed, even though Lala told me that—at some point—kids needed to learn how to figure out their gag reflex and swallow on their own. It made sense to me, rationally speaking, but it was scary to think about putting it into practice.

I couldn't imagine how Lala, or anyone for that matter, could be such a calm parent. But Brittany was the same way. She loved being a mom and never seemed to be bothered by anything, whereas for me, motherhood was the most distressing thing I'd ever experienced. Brock was also a very chill parent. I'd just chalked that up to the difference between men and women. He hadn't suffered a miscarriage or almost died during childbirth. Despite having all these people in my corner, I felt totally isolated and like I was the only one having these tormenting thoughts.

As I spent more and more time with Lala and Brittany, I began to consider how I could be more like them as a mom, especially when I began to realize where my neuroses came from. Growing up, my own mother had always been there to catch me before I fell. I felt like I'd been coddled my whole life. I barely got hurt, except when I broke my nose playing baseball when I was eight, but there was nothing anyone could have done to prevent that. Aside from my nose, I was never seriously injured. It was like I lived in a little bubble protected by my mom.

Believe me, I would have loved to keep Summer in a bubble, too—so I could see where my mom was coming from. But I knew I needed to give her the tools to fall on her own when I wasn't around. She also had to learn how to brush herself off and recover. My helicopter attitude was unhealthy for both of us, and I had to ease up. Even when we did something as low stakes as go to the park, I was always constantly hovering over her, so I started trying to stay a few paces behind her instead. I understood that she wasn't going to have me there every step of the way for her whole life, even though I really wanted to be.

Once I was able to relax a little, I also felt compelled to open up to my therapist about how far apart Lala and I were as moms. I thought, how can I be more like her when I'm envisioning worst-case scenarios in my head? That was when she told me that I likely had postpartum OCD. I had no idea that was a thing. I'd always thought that OCD meant obsessive organization and a fear of germs, like Howie Mandel and Khloe Kardashian. I never knew that intrusive thoughts were also a symptom. In fact, I didn't even call them that.

This movie, *Role Models*, has a scene where Jane Lynch is sitting at her desk, and she points to her head and says, "I used to have sick thoughts." When I saw that, I realized that was me. I always called my thoughts sick, as opposed to intrusive, which is a much gentler and more forgiving term.

I remember at my six-week postbirth checkup, the doctor had given me a questionnaire with fifteen questions about postpartum depression. There were definitely a few I'd wanted to answer yes to, but I'd read a lot about PPD—enough to know that it wasn't exactly what I had. So, I lied a bit on the form, because I didn't want to be misdiagnosed or medicated for the wrong thing.

When I shared this with my therapist a year later, she said that postpartum OCD is often misdiagnosed as postpartum depression, as many physicians don't know enough about it. Then she asked how I was with numbers. I thought that was an interesting question, because—immediately—something clicked for me. I told her that, for about a decade, I'd been following precisely 420 people on Instagram. I'd formerly been a massive stoner, and it was a sort of lucky number for me. This meant that when I met someone new and wanted to follow them on IG, I had to unfollow someone else. There were actually people who reached out to me because they'd noticed that I'd unfollowed them and wanted to know if we were in a fight. I was too chicken to admit the real reason why I'd unfollowed them so I'd concoct some bizarre lie, like that my sister had gone through my followers and might have thought that their account was inactive. I had so many canned excuses that made no sense at all.

Incidentally, my mom did the same thing. She followed 333 people, because it was an angel number that symbolized divine love, protection, and presence. Now she's over 500 (good job, Mom!).

Obviously, I realized that my obsession with the number 420 wasn't normal, but I couldn't shake it, and it was something strangers came to know about me. People would alert me via DM if my number somehow crept up to 421. And I was thankful for this—for ten full years.

It wasn't just limited to IG. When I was driving in my car,

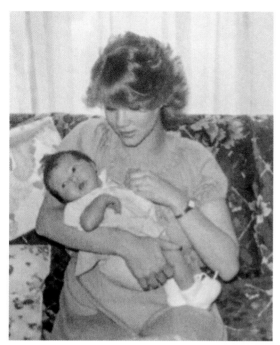

My mom brought me home from the hospital on Mother's Day, 1985. She turned twenty a few days later.

This photo, my first pic with my dad, was taken in my maternal grandparents' living room in Azusa, California, which is now my parents' house.

As you can see, from a young age, I always liked to keep things tidy. I wish I still had "Jennifer Bunny" because she went everywhere with me.

The late '80s and early '90s was all about dance for me! I had dance recitals at Finkbiner Park in Glendora, California, where I performed tap and jazz routines in those early years. Can you see the Paula Abdul vision?

I always loved dressing up for Halloween. I may not have been a Witch of WeHo, but I was a Witch of Azusa in 1990.

While playing baseball on the all-boys' team, I was the second baseman—or rather, *basewoman*—and loved every minute of it.

I was extremely close with Papa and Puna, my maternal grandparents. They lived nearby, which meant I got to see them almost daily.

Aunt Shirley, my cousin Genesis, and I shortly after I started playing baseball at one of the annual luaus my grandparents hosted. Aunt Shirley was a legend and every time I saw her as a kid I got starstruck.

Meeting my little sister, Cortney, for the very first time. Our family finally felt complete.

My childhood best friend Gina Marie and I went to have our "star shots" taken at the local mall. Hey, in 1997 Azusa, this was absolutely the look.

Working at the Irwindale Speedway as "Miss Mopar" my senior year of high school.

Gloria Allred, my friend Brooke, and me posing for a photo during a media trip to New York City in 2004 to share our experiences of being secretly videotaped during a job interview at Hooters.

JC Chasez and me hanging at his house in 2005. We met out one night at a club called LAX. I hadn't even graduated college yet and was using a fake ID to get into the LA clubs.

This is the last photo I have with Gina Marie before she passed away from cancer at the young age of twenty-three. Shortly before she gained her wings, she gifted me the love frog plush that accompanies me everywhere I go. I love that she continues to share in my life and adventures in that way.

In Dante Basco's trailer on the set of the movie *Biker Boyz*. My friend Brooke and I were extras, but we made friends with the cast. It was my first time on a movie set and in a talent trailer, but I knew it wouldn't be my last.

With Raul, my biological father, at his office in Las Vegas sometime in the mid-to-late aughts, based on my attire. One regret Raul said he has is that we didn't take many photos together growing up, but that's also because he said he was always living in the moment.

"Maria the Pizza Girl" in a Jonas Brothers sandwich while filming Disney's *Jonas* with Kevin, Joe, and Nick in late 2008. To date, this was one of the most fun acting jobs I've ever had.

On the set of *Victorious* circa 2010. I played an actress who needed a stunt double, played by Victoria Justice. Can you tell who is who?

One of the most fun things Eddie and I would do together was take his boat out with friends. The only ring in that boat was a life preserver, so word to the wise, ladies—if a man tells you he's separated, don't believe him.

I loved my Villa Blanca family. Here I am with some of the crew who came out to support me for my show at the Roxy, which was featured on *VPR* during season 1.

At the LA County Fair in 2014 with Shay, Katie, Ariana, and the Toms. I have attended every year since I was born.

BTS of *VPR* season 7 in Puerto Vallarta with Brittany and Ariana. I was so happy when these girls joined the cast, in seasons 4 and 2, respectively. I finally felt like I had fellow females on the show who had my back.

Some of the best memories from my time working at SUR and filming for *VPR* were celebrating Pride. Here I am with Katie, Stassi, Kristen, Lala, and Brittany during the 2018 festival.

My first photo with Brock at the KAABOO music festival in Del Mar, California, in 2019. We had only met the night before but there was definitely a spark.

Six weeks after meeting, Brock asked me to meet him on the other side of the world. Just eight months prior, I was passing through Sydney's Harbour Bridge on a girls trip. I fell in love with Australia, and then fell for an Australian.

Pregnant with my rainbow baby in March 2021. I had a feeling I may not be able to carry another child so I took an insane amount of maternity photos, and I'm so happy I did because my intuition was right.
(Photo credit: Mona Marandy)

The most perfect baby in the world was born on April 26, 2021, at 5:11 a.m. This moment of bliss was short-lived, though, as my pre-eclampsia had advanced to HELLP Syndrome, and I was rushed to the high-risk ICU.

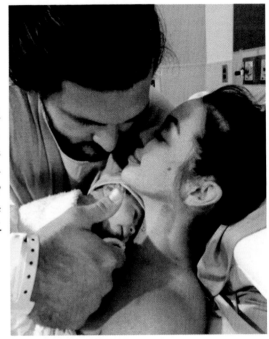

Having Summer as our flower girl at my and Brock's second wedding was so special. Right before I walked down the aisle, a rainbow appeared in the sky, and I knew the baby we lost was there in spirit. *(Photo Credit: Morgan Taylor)*

Lala, Brittany, Stassi, and me with the babes. Our first outing all together at the Grove, and the fact that we were able to get a picture of us four looking decent with all the kids, was nothing short of a miracle!

Christmas Day 2024 in Palm Springs, California. Mom, Dad, Cortney, Justice, Brock, Summer, and Riley the pup. Celebrating Christmas in the desert with my next-door neighbor, Lala Kent, and her family has become a nice holiday tradition.

BTS of *VPR* season 11 with the girls: Ally, Lala, Katie, and Ariana. We were going for a retro look that night at Hotel Ziggy.

And I finally got my very own trailer! Here I am with my mom on set for season 13 of *The Masked Singer*. As someone who is not a trained (or naturally gifted) vocalist, singing live on national television was not something I ever planned to do again, but I had a great time and am proud of myself for stepping outside of my comfort zone.

I'd have to crank the volume up on the radio until I saw four small lines and a single tall one on the display. It couldn't be under or over. Additionally, my TV volume had to be set at an odd number. It couldn't be 24 or 26. It had to be 23, 25, or 27, and this was all based on absolutely nothing. Just a feeling I had.

When I finally confessed all of this to my therapist, she was certain that I had postpartum OCD, which she informed me was mild to moderate, not severe, as it wasn't completely debilitating. Soon, a psychiatrist also confirmed this diagnosis, which lifted such a weight off me. After months of feeling alone with my thoughts, I finally understood what was wrong.

With that said, it was still impacting my everyday life, and it needed to be treated. My therapist proceeded to tell me about exposure and response prevention, a behavioral therapy that treats OCD by helping patients gradually face their fears and resist compulsions. She also suggested cognitive behavioral therapy, which is a short-term, goal-oriented, and structured psychotherapy that can help with a variety of mental and physical health issues. Another option was to have a psychiatrist prescribe medication, but that wasn't my default preference, so I wasn't into that idea even though I had taken them in the past.

Fortunately, my therapist understood my resistance to medication and said that a fourth possibility was eye movement desensitization and reprocessing (EMDR)—a psychotherapy technique that can help people heal from trauma and distressing life experiences. I'd heard of EMDR before, so I took a few months to think about it and, ultimately, was willing to try it. At first, we did it over Zoom, which wasn't effective. Eventually, we attempted the treatment in person, and it started to make a difference.

Around the same time, I attended a movie premiere, where I met two girls who'd been on *Big Brother*. My sister was a fan of the show, and it turned out they were fans of mine. We had a great conversation, and I really liked them. Of course, this led to them following me on IG and, even though I knew that it would raise my number to 422, I followed them on the spot. I wasn't prepared to tell them I couldn't follow them because of my strange issue with numbers. And I left it that way for the rest of the night.

Did I have the strong urge to unfollow two people the next day? Yes, I did. But I couldn't find two people whom I felt comfortable letting go. So, I simply didn't. And, after that, one by one, I followed even more people until it didn't matter to me anymore. I realized that by holding on to this 420 number I was preventing myself from making and maintaining real connections, which I no longer wanted to do.

Shortly thereafter, I shared my progress with my therapist, and she told me that I'd accomplished exposure therapy. She said the fact that I'd done it on my own, without her prompts, was huge. I felt so proud of myself, and thought, Okay, what's next? Now I could follow even more people and listen to the TV at whatever volume I liked. As simple as these accomplishments might sound, I was going through this total awakening. Finally, I was able to comprehend that nothing bad would happen if I followed nine hundred people or adjusted the TV volume to an even number. No one was putting a gun to my head if I stepped out of my comfort zone. It was one of the most freeing things I'd ever experienced. It reminded me of when I was a kid, and words of affirmation made me want to be better at whatever it was I'd set my mind to.

My therapist then asked me what I was most afraid to do with Summer. On a scale of 1 to 10, what was my level 10? I said it was either going to Disneyland or flying somewhere, just the two of us. Those were my two biggest fears, as I was scared to simply be alone with her and especially to be alone in public. I was terrified that if something bad happened to Summer, my maternal instincts wouldn't kick in and I wouldn't know what to do. So, despite my progress, these two things still seemed very daunting.

But I was determined to keep getting better. So I decided to take Summer to Disneyland by myself. My mom asked if she could come and help, but—as tempted as I was to say yes—I realized it was something I needed to do on my own. Fortunately, I knew a little hack for the best place to park that made it easier with a stroller, especially because it was a particularly busy day at Disney. The lines were so long that, while we were waiting to go on Monsters, Inc., Summer was understandably impatient and ducking under the bars that kept people in the queue, which really stressed me out. I could feel my anxiety mounting. At that point, I decided to call a friend who worked there. She said that she was at the princess brunch at the Grand California Hotel and that if we hurried over, she could hold all the princesses for Summer to have a private meeting with them, which was truly awesome. She also gave us FastPasses so we could go back to Monsters, Inc., along with the Little Mermaid ride and many others, without Summer getting impatient. Having the stress of managing Summer in line lifted made a huge difference.

Finally, after five hours, I was exhausted and ready to leave. Then my sister called me and asked if I wanted her to meet us.

I said yes, only if she could get there quickly, which she did. Thankfully, when she arrived, I got to sit down for the first time and eat some food. I also got to go to the bathroom by myself. Since Summer was only two, still in diapers, it had been impossible for me to do that without some help. We wrapped up the day with five more rides thanks to my sister's assistance. I recorded a vlog about the whole thing and was so proud of myself for not only surviving but also for conquering my fear.

I truly didn't think I'd ever be able to be alone with Summer at Disneyland, but I did it, and I was very proud of my evolution. Seeing that I had it in myself to grow and to push past what made me uncomfortable gave me a lot of confidence. You miss 100 percent of the shots you don't take. And unless you face your fears, they will always remain simply that—fears. Finally, I felt like the mom who could have fun mom-daughter days and not be so scared. After this success, I continue to work on different forms of exposure therapy in an attempt to overcome my demons.

Since then, I've also gotten involved with the International OCD Foundation (IOCDF), which has allowed me to help women just like me to understand what's happening with them, that there's a name for what they're enduring, and there are means to treat it. Thankfully, I eventually got to share some of my postpartum OCD journey on season eleven.

I credit that opportunity to the fact that, for season ten, we got a new showrunner. He had worked on the show for the first eight seasons, was a husband and a father, and was interested in embracing the genuine stories of our lives as parents and human beings. I couldn't have been happier with this decision, because the former showrunner, who'd been with us for nine seasons, was never interested in highlighting our emotional journeys; all he cared about was the petty drama.

But the reality was that our audience had grown with all of us through the years and the new showrunner saw, as we did, that they wanted to connect with us during the bigger, deeper, more honest moments. It was both comforting and inspiring that we could finally shine a spotlight on issues like women's health and postpartum journeys. I knew these topics would be so relatable to the majority of our viewers, who were mostly female.

More than three million people in the United States alone suffer from OCD, and it's upward of 150 million worldwide. I truly never realized how substantial the statistics were. Receiving the Illumination Award from the IOCDF was the highest honor, as I was awarded for being *me* and for speaking out about a subject that's often taboo or has a stigma attached to it.

Going through this experience has changed my perspective on what it means to be a reality TV star, and having the platform and opportunity to raise awareness is deeply meaningful.

I've had so many people reach out to me to say that they now understand what's wrong with them and they're seeking help. When I hear that someone was suicidal and that listening to me talk about mental health encouraged them to get help, it reinforces my commitment to make a difference. I know I'm on the right path.

While I may never be entirely cured, I'm blown away by the amount of progress I've made, and I couldn't be prouder to provide important representation for everyone, especially new moms struggling with the same affliction.

13

THE PROPOSAL

B y July 2021, three months after Summer was born, Brock and I had already lived through the pandemic and had a baby together, so we were committed to making our family work. The next obvious steps were engagement and marriage. Brock wanted to do both on the show because, given my history with men and the way I'd been presented on *VPR* (first as a home-wrecking whore and later as a pick-me girl), he wanted the world to see that I was truly loved.

The original plan for the proposal was that Brock would enlist Randall's help to set up a fake movie screening, so that I had a legitimate reason to get glammed up without suspicion. Then, all of a sudden, the curtain would go up and start playing a montage of our relationship, including many of the special moments and milestones we'd shared. Our friends and family were going to be there, ready to surprise me, and as soon as the montage was over, Brock was not only going to propose, but he was going to have an officiant on hand to marry us right then and there.

Unfortunately, a number of things went wrong with his plan. First, there was a permit issue with the venue. Then, since this was still during the pandemic, everything had to be outdoors, which impacted the capacity for guests. And, finally, there was an issue with the caterer. Production kept trying to get Brock to change venues, but the alternates they suggested didn't work for a few reasons. Either it was someplace Brock knew I wouldn't like, or it was a location I'd made memories at with another guy.

Regardless, the show was hoping to film the proposal, especially because part of season nine's story line was already based around it. So, Brock felt extremely pressured to do something amazing in a short amount of time, as our wrap date was quickly approaching. Additionally, our cast trip for the finale was going to be centered on James and Raquel's engagement party, so he didn't want to overshadow that, or lead people to believe that I was trying to make everything about me.

Ultimately, Brock decided to do something more private, since there were too many complications. His love language is acts of service, and he's amazing with grand gestures—he goes big or he goes home, and he doesn't like to fail at things, certainly not at planning a perfect, magical proposal. He also realized that our actual relationship was most important above all else, including getting the right narrative for the show.

Brock ended up proposing on the balcony of our apartment with a 12.74-carat cushion-cut pink morganite ring set in a

14-carat white gold band with diamonds, designed by jeweler Kyle Chan. There were gold and white balloon arches with a sign that said MARRY ME, and red and white rose petals covering the floor.

While holding my hands, Brock said, "You make me the best, and I don't want to do anything without you ever. You are the best mom. You are the best girlfriend, and I want to make you the best wife." I laughed softly, as he got down on one knee and asked, "Honey, will you be my wife?" I said, "Of course!" It was truly perfect. Summer was there as well, and it was so intimate.

Earlier that day we'd met our attorneys downstairs in the conference room to sign our prenup—it was a bit unorthodox as we didn't have a wedding date set, but we wanted all of our ducks in a row (marriage license included) so that we could get married whenever we wanted to, even if it was on a whim. Since we'd just had a business type of meeting with our attorneys, I was dressed more conservatively than I would have liked for proposal pictures. So, we re-created them later that evening with me in a white dress.

A few days after we got engaged, we were ready to travel to Solvang, a city in southern California's Santa Ynez Valley, for James and Raquel's engagement party at Sunstone Winery on Sunday, July 18, 2021. It was going to be the last night of filming for season nine.

What no one knew (including me, at first) was that the plan was for me and Brock to have a secret elopement while we were there, without alerting the rest of the cast. At this point, Brock had to let me in on the idea, because I needed a dress, and he knew I'd want to be involved in some of the planning. I was actually cool with it. I'd already had a big wedding, and all I cared about was marrying Brock. We also decided to include Tom and Ariana in our secret, as we were going to need some help pulling it off.

The plan was that once we got to Solvang, we were all going to do different activities. Some people would go horseback riding with Lisa, while others would go on a boat ride. Meanwhile, Tom and Ariana would come with us to do an activity that no one would know about. My parents were going to be there as well. And Brock's family was going to Zoom in from Australia. I packed my dress and was prepared to marry my man.

When we arrived in Solvang, it was suggested that our nuptials take place on the property where James and Raquel were staying, which had a massive, beautiful chateau. Immediately, I said, "No way. I'm not getting married on the morning of Raquel's engagement party in the exact same spot. She's going to be standing on her balcony and realize there are cameras filming us saying our vows! Not happening." I put my foot down and said, "This isn't what I want, and I'm not doing it." I had so much anxiety, and nothing about it felt right.

In light of my feelings, one of our new producers—who worked on the show for only that season—came up with a compromise. Since we were no longer getting married, the deal was that we were going to announce our engagement the night before the engagement party. The problem was that filming for that night ended up being canceled due to COVID issues, so it had to happen the next day—the same day as the engagement party—while we were visiting an alpaca farm. Basically, it would look like I was making James and Raquel's engagement about me, which wasn't at all surprising. I'd been in the same situation many times before. But, I agreed, as long as James and Raquel were not going to be there. I didn't want to ruin their special day. I figured I'd tell them privately.

So, off we went to the alpaca farm, where we stood up, gave a champagne toast, and shared our exciting news with the entire cast, except James and Raquel. What's strange is that, in the moment, I thought everyone was congratulatory and genuinely happy for us. Yet, when I watched it back a few months later, I saw that the general reaction was disgust. There were a few eye rolls and pinched noses. Cut to their interviews, where people said things like, "Scheana is so tacky. How could she do that?" We were portrayed as inconsiderate and classless, which made me feel taken advantage of once again.

When we were leaving the alpaca farm, Lala said to me, "I've got to tell you something. I'm getting pressure to bring up your engagement at James and Raquel's party tonight. This is being put all on me. You and I have made so much progress in our friendship and we're finally in a good place. I don't want to do it."

Brock and I both agreed. We didn't want Lala to be the bearer of the news, either. At the same time, we were all under a lot of pressure to produce an explosive finale, and we knew all of our jobs were kind of on the line if we didn't deliver. So, I said, "Why don't we have Katie be the one to tell them? I'd much rather fight with her." Lala loved that idea. As did Ariana, whom we let in on the plan.

Predictably, Katie was into it, too, as she was always game to pick a fight with me. Everyone was happy. That was until Katie got overserved and couldn't see straight. I swear if someone had asked her, she probably couldn't even remember her name. I knew there was no way she was going to be able to pull things off and get her points across.

Instead Lala, who was of course completely sober, was going to tell James and Raquel that Brock and I were trying to get engaged at their party. And, as a result of this bombshell, drama would ensue and hopefully guarantee another season. Job security, check! It would feel like a moment where we all ended up making great TV.

The amusing thing was that at the end of the night, I went back to the hotel in the same car as Brock and Lala. I remember Charli seeing us leave together. She was so confused because we'd all been fighting and then we were peacefully driving away together. But we didn't care. We'd fulfilled our self-imposed assignment and were proud of ourselves.

Ultimately, the producers were thrilled to have their dramatic finale. The engagement party was a bust. James's mom was royally pissed. James and Raquel didn't work out as a couple anyway, and we all got another season out of it, which definitely was not guaranteed prior to our little plan.

After that, the attention turned to my and Brock's wedding. One of our producers told us, in no uncertain terms, that they really wanted us to get married on camera because it was going to be a story line. I was afraid to be demoted if I didn't comply, so, after filming wrapped for season nine, I went to production and said, "Look, we need to get married on paper in order to get Brock's green card process going. We're just going to have a private little ceremony and not tell anyone about it. If you guys want to have a big wedding on the show, we can still do that. But legally, we'll already be married." They agreed, as long as we kept our mouths shut with the cast and our friends, which we did.

Brock and I officially became husband and wife on August 28, 2021, at our home in San Diego.

My cousin David—the one who bought me the pager when I was being bullied in junior high—married us, which he's now technically done three times (Shay once and Brock twice). My parents and two of David's kids were there, as were Cortney and her boyfriend, Justice. Brock's mom was on Zoom. We said our vows and took photos. We even filmed the whole thing, in case production ever wanted to use any of it on the show, which they did not. (It was, however, posted on my Patreon as a little exclusive.) And that was fine with me, because it was such an intimate, special day. I knew Brock was my person. We'd created a family together, and we didn't need to shout our love to the world. We were happy to keep the moment for ourselves and our family. Besides, it was kind of fun to have a little secret.

Around the same time, during the season nine reunion, James and Raquel called off their engagement. Raquel wanted to move out immediately, and, understanding her pain, I offered her our beautiful penthouse apartment in Hollywood while Brock and I lived in our house in San Diego during the off-season. She was very grateful and I was more than happy to do it, which goes to show that our friendships are not just for the cameras; they exist in real life, too. I really wanted to support Raquel during a tough time in her life. She stayed in our place for over five months.

I had no clue that living in San Diego would lead to me being demoted for season ten. Production claimed it was because I'd said something on my podcast about not residing in LA, which was what *VPR* was based around. Though I think the main reason was because Brock's past, with his ex and older children, resonated poorly with the audience.

Either way, I was dropped down to a day rate again, but with a 5 percent increase from the last one. And they said I would still be part of the main cast, but that they didn't care to have Brock around. It was fine if he wanted to be part of group stuff, but they just wouldn't be giving him call times.

I was pissed. It felt like a total fuck-you, especially because Brock had put himself out there for season nine, for zero pay, only to be eviscerated on national television. And all so I could get demoted for the following season.

At that point, there was no way we were having our wedding on TV. We were already married, and the producers were acting like they weren't interested in us anyway. We'd thought about doing another small thing in Bali or Australia, but—in part, because we were living on only my income, which had just been reduced—we eventually landed on an all-inclusive resort in Mexico. COVID restrictions and the ease of travel with a baby in tow also played a role in our decision.

Once production got wind of those plans, suddenly they were interested in filming the wedding and said they'd double my day rate for each day we were in Mexico. Obviously, they were cool with Brock being a major part of it, since he was the groom!

Even though I didn't feel like the show recognized my worth and my confidence had been beaten down, I was the sole provider for my family and the people on the cast were my legitimate friends, so I decided to take the check and do what I had to do—another televised wedding.

This time around, I knew I needed a full-blown planner. I did not want another shit show, like the first time with Shay. Thankfully, a friend recommended a great woman named

Shelby from Simply Classic Events, who specialized in destination weddings. We ultimately landed on Dreams Natura Resort & Spa in Cancún, Mexico, with her guidance. I told Shelby I wanted to keep the guest list tight—under a hundred people, if not under fifty. And we needed to be able to film at the venue.

We decided to do it on a Tuesday, which we figured would make it inconvenient for many, and thereby lower the number of attendees and the cost. Of course, we still ended up with 120 and easily could have had 150, but I drew the line at twelve tables of ten. I cut all plus-ones who'd recently started dating, and—at first—one of those people was James's new girlfriend, Ally Lewber. I had no way of knowing if they'd stay together, and I barely knew her. I said she could come to the welcome party and the after-party, but not the actual wedding.

Fortunately, it worked out that she ended up coming to the wedding anyway, as we became fast friends, and I invited her on my bachelorette trip. Ally and I have been very close ever since, so I'm happy she was able to be there.

This time around, the wedding—and the entire weekend—was perfect. I didn't have to think about a single detail. There was such a different wave of emotions and feelings, because I felt like Brock was the right man for me, no questions or concerns. And it felt special to say our vows for the second time, in front of all of our friends and family. I didn't feel any pressure, since Brock and I were already legally married. It was kind of exciting that I had that secret, though I did tell my bridesmaids the night before that we were technically celebrating our one-year anniversary. They couldn't believe I'd kept it under wraps for so long!

I couldn't have asked for a more perfect day. Honestly, the

welcome party almost topped the main event, as there were fire dancers, water drums, and swings in the swimming pool with this 360-degree camera that captured it all.

During the ceremony, the only thing that wasn't ideal was the wind, as it blew my very long veil off my head. (Although it made for one incredible photo later.) Naturally, my good side was toward the audience when it happened, and the photographer suggested I face the other way in order to keep the veil in place. If you've been following my journey through the years, you know how much I *love* my good side, but I told myself it didn't matter because I was marrying my person, and that was the most important thing above all else. Regardless, when I switched sides, the veil was still blowing off, so I gave it to my sister to hold. Everyone was surprised at how casual I was about the whole thing, as I'm usually such a perfectionist. But I was so full of joy that day, the little hiccups didn't matter.

The most beautiful moment was when I was walking down the aisle, with Israel Kamakawiwoʻole's version of "Somewhere over the Rainbow" playing. Israel was a Hawaiian singer, and my grandparents used to live in Hawaii. When I was growing up, we had a luau every Memorial Day weekend until Papa passed away, so that song was very special to me. Right as it began playing, a rainbow appeared in the sky. And I felt the baby we had lost was there with us in spirit. My amazing rainbow baby, Summer, was actually present, scattering rose petals down the aisle. What was remarkable was that the ceremony started twenty minutes late, and if it hadn't, we would have missed the rainbow. It couldn't have been more serendipitous.

Following the ceremony, we had the most fun reception and after-party, with all of my close friends, my family, Brock's family, and spectacular fireworks in the sky. Brock and I had our *Dirty Dancing* moment (the first dance), which was reminiscent of when we initially met and went to the music festival in San Diego. We'd only practiced it once, and I'd never done it in six-inch heels and a heavily beaded dress. But I used my core to help hoist myself into the air and, once I was up there, all of these fire sparklers went off. We nailed it!

One strange thing that went down was when my wedding dress designer's husband informed me that he'd seen Tom and Raquel making out by the elevators. I just assumed he meant Tom Schwartz, because they'd kissed at the welcome party, and because Tom Sandoval was dating Ariana. What we didn't yet know was that Raquel and Tom Sandoval had sex on that trip and were sneaking around behind Ariana's back, which was so messy.

What I did know was that Katie Maloney was on-site, even though she wasn't invited to the wedding. She was upset with me as she believed I was setting up her ex (Tom Schwartz) with Raquel. Believing that she didn't wish me well, her presence felt like a dark cloud of energy lurking around the property. To be fair, it was a filmed trip, so I understood why she was there (to guarantee her episodic paycheck at my expense). I was actually fine with her coming to Mexico…until the resort was sold out and I needed her room and she refused to give it up, despite my offer to reimburse her more than market value, claiming she deserved this "vacation." Yet I didn't deserve to go to Havasu on her girls' trip earlier in the season and collect my day rates for that week, when she was well aware that less filming would mean less income for me and my family. That exclusion felt pettier than any other I've experienced throughout my years of filming the show, as the intent wasn't to ostracize me from the other female cast, it was to reduce my paycheck. And while we might have crossed many lines over the years, messing with another's business, their finances, was a new low among the cast.

In hindsight, I wish Katie and I had been able to have a calm, mature conversation about the fact that she'd recently gotten divorced from Schwartz and was in a bad place. Our relationship was probably the worst it's ever been in those months. She felt that I took Tom's side in the divorce because I had him on my podcast. However, she never listened to that episode. If she had, she would have heard me coming to her defense and having her back. That was also the first time production had ever agreed to cover my podcast on the show. It took ten seasons for an outside project of mine to be highlighted, aside from my music hobby! It felt like instead of listening, she just reacted and made certain assumptions. That drove us further apart and made me not want to show up for her. However, when I watched the show back, I saw how broken she was, and I realized that I should have been the bigger person.

Besides that tension and Tom Sandoval and Raquel's betrayal, which I didn't yet know about, the wedding went off without a hitch. Once it was over, we returned to our lives in LA and finished filming season ten. I was ready to start the rest of my life with Brock and Summer and finally have my happily ever after.

14

SOMETHING BORROWED

Going into 2023, I was ready for change. Brock and I were fresh off of our wedding in Mexico, and after years of fighting for my place within the *VPR* friend group, I genuinely had true bonds with Tom, Ariana, Raquel, and Lala. I was still on a day rate, but I'd received double pay for each day of our wedding, and the show was featuring Brock more. So, I felt like production finally realized that our story was still an integral part of the show, which was somewhat validating. That being said, it seemed like *VPR* was winding down, and Brock and I had started discussing what our next chapter would be. We were hopeful and excited for the future, thinking about another possible show, continuing to grow my podcast, and focusing on building our brand as a family. Brock is a big dreamer, which means we're always batting around new ideas.

In light of this long-awaited enthusiasm and optimism, I definitely didn't expect for everyone's worlds to be blown up on March 1, with the eruption of Scandoval.

I think it's fair to say that I'm not always the best judge of character, and I have a blind spot for taking people at their word, especially when it comes to relationships—whether platonic or romantic. But one thing I pride myself on, even if it gets me in trouble at times, is that I'm a firm believer in giving people the benefit of the doubt. This means that sometimes, I afford people too many chances (like Eddie and Shay). It's the way my mom raised me—to always put others first, to understand that everyone is human, and to realize that we all make mistakes, which may not define who we are. Yet, no matter how many times I've been burned, I haven't been jaded from trying to see the best in others.

Tom and Raquel's secret affair was a prime example, one that would ultimately reverberate, not just among my castmates, but across the globe.

While we were filming season ten, the rumors began to circulate that Tom was cheating on Ariana—his girlfriend of nearly a decade—with Raquel. Katie and Lala were the leaders of the pack, insinuating that Raquel was the type of girl to go after someone else's man. At the time, I thought they were overreacting, because I couldn't believe Raquel and Tom would ever do that to Ariana. Raquel was one of our closest friends and Tom and Ariana had been in a long-term, serious relationship; it was the ultimate betrayal. Honestly, I thought that kind of thing only happened in movies, not in real life and certainly not in my friend group.

Beyond Katie and Lala's gossip, Ally Lewber also witnessed Tom and Raquel's connection at the Abbey in West Hollywood in September 2022, shortly after my wedding to Brock. She'd alerted a few of us at the time, though it didn't air on *VPR* until April 2023, a month after Scandoval broke—when Ally said, "I saw Sandoval and Raquel dancing together at the Abbey after See You Next Tuesday," which was an event at SUR. She then added, "I personally wouldn't be comfortable to have my boyfriend out at 1 a.m. with girls."

So, before anyone could confirm the affair, the intimacy that Ally witnessed was the smoking gun, and her discomfort with Tom and Raquel's PDA made Katie and Lala even more suspicious. They couldn't understand why other people weren't recognizing the same thing.

For my part, I'll admit I had some serious blinders on. As I said, I thought Tom and Raquel were good people and would never hurt Ariana like that. When Ally told me about her inkling, I replied that she was new to the group and didn't understand their close friendship. I thought she was just stirring the pot. I explained that the simple act of them dancing together was not a big deal and that she was dramatizing an innocent situation. I'd danced with Sandoval at the Abbey when Ariana wasn't there, so it didn't feel shady to me. Ariana was way more of a homebody than Tom, which meant that he was often out with friends, including Raquel, while Ariana was happily back at the house they shared, doing her own thing.

Ally then asked, "It wouldn't bother you if that had been Brock and Raquel?" I replied, "No. There's nothing weird about it. I would trust Brock in the same bed as Raquel. Let's stop making this a thing, because now it's just fueling Lala and Katie's distrust. Tom and Raquel would never do that."

Ally heard what I was saying and apologized for being

suspicious, recognizing that she didn't know them super well. She didn't want to spread rumors, either. I told her it was okay, but not to bring it up again. Tom and Raquel were friends. That was it.

The fact that Raquel and Tom Schwartz had kissed at my wedding also reassured me that nothing shady was going on with her and Sandoval. And Raquel had doubled down on Schwartz by insisting that she was so into him, despite the fact that she was already secretly hooking up with Sandoval at that point. *Gross.* In hindsight, Raquel and Sandoval clearly hatched this plan to get people off their scent.

With gossip still swirling, season ten wrapped in mid-September. Three months later, on New Year's Eve, I was at Schwartz & Sandy's with Brock, our friends Will and Elaine, Raquel, Schwartz, Sandoval, and Ariana. I remember Raquel saying that she was hoping to be Schwartz's midnight kiss. They'd even exchanged a text about it. I thought that was cute, since they'd already kissed, and I still felt like they had chemistry. According to Raquel, the plan was that she would find Schwartz a few minutes before midnight so they could lock lips. But, once midnight rolled around, Schwartz was out of sight, hiding in the bathroom because he didn't want to make out with her. I assumed that was just Schwartz being Schwartz, because he can be skittish when it comes to stuff like that. He's never been someone who steps up to the plate when it comes to women. Even though he's cute, charismatic, charming, and intelligent, he doesn't have a lot of game. When a pretty girl comes around, he gets insecure and runs away.

Although, in retrospect, I'm guessing he knew about Raquel and Sandoval and didn't want to be directly involved in their affair.

Meanwhile, everyone else there was coupled up, and I felt

badly for Raquel. After I kissed Brock, I kissed Raquel. It was the one time Brock was sort of okay with it, because it was a pity kiss, not a sexually charged make-out. We were all best friends and one big happy family, so it was cool. It felt really good to be in an intimate setting, surrounded by the people closest to me, and married to the man I loved.

As the bar was closing down and we were all figuring out where to go next, Sandoval suggested having everyone over to his and Ariana's house. Predictably, Ariana did not want that. She just wanted to go home and be with Tom because their anniversary was New Year's Day, and it was a very important time for them. She was clearly annoyed, and I understood her frustration. Tom is the guy who always wants to keep the party going, whereas Ariana wanted to be alone with her boyfriend, who—unbeknownst to her—wanted to be around Raquel.

They then started fighting about it at the bar with raised voices. I wasn't completely shocked, though it was the first time in a while that I'd seen big cracks in their relationship. It made me sad because I always thought they were a solid couple, and I had a feeling something more was up. I pulled Ariana aside, and asked if things were okay between them.

"No, they're not good," she admitted.

I said, "I get that. Let's hang out this weekend and talk about it. I want to be there for you."

She agreed to hang out and reiterated that she was pissed with Tom. And I responded, "Don't worry; we're not coming to your house. I'm rallying the group to go to an after-party on the west side. I'm sure you guys will work through it." The rest of us headed out, and I hoped Ariana and Tom would both cool off once they got home.

Shortly thereafter, Janet revealed to me there was a night in the beginning of January when a few people got together at her house. Apparently, while Raquel and Sandoval were outside alone together, someone commented to Ariana about their closeness. Ariana stormed outside and said, "I'm sick of hearing that people think there's something going on between the two of you. Get your shit together and stop it." I believed then, and believe now, that Ariana didn't suspect something was going on. She just wanted them to stop feeding the chatter, which I could understand. As someone whose relationships had been picked apart, I knew what it was like to feel like you were under a microscope.

Of course it didn't end there. Later that month, I started taking dance classes with Raquel and our friend Jenny Ting. After the second class, we decided to go out for dinner and Raquel said, "I know these two bar owners who have a place in West Hollywood called TomTom; should we go there?" She played it off like she was joking, since we all knew Sandoval and Schwartz, but we went anyway, as it was close by. It turned out Tom and Tom were not in house that night.

I'm not sure what prompted me to do this, but I shared with Jenny that people were suspicious of Raquel and Sandoval. She'd known Raquel and her family since they were teenagers, and I guess I thought she might be able to see something that I didn't. I said, "Ariana thinks nothing's going on, but I have a strange feeling. Can you help me figure out if Raquel is hiding something?" Jenny agreed.

Throughout dinner, we questioned Raquel about how much she was hanging out with Tom until finally she said, "Tom is my best friend. I'm closer with him than I am with Ariana at this point. And he wants to break up with Ariana. But every time he's tried to bring it up, she threatens to kill herself."

As one of Ariana's closest friends, I knew she'd been struggling with mental health issues for a long time and that she'd had ideations of suicide, so immediately, I was concerned.

Raquel went on to disclose that things were really bad between Ariana and Sandoval, which made me even more worried. I said, "Look, I get that you guys are really tight, but is there something more to it?" She shook her head. I continued, "To be clear, you're telling me nothing's happened with you and Tom, right? He's never made a move on you, nothing physical, you guys have never even kissed?" She replied, "God, no. As I said, he's my best friend. He feels comfortable confiding in me. I'm just there to listen." Raquel was so adamant about it that I wanted to believe her, but instead I said, "Do you want something to happen?" Suddenly, her face looked like the happy tear emoji on the iPhone. My antennae went up, and I pressed her again with, "Raquel, are you in love with Sandoval?" She swore that she was not. But I wasn't sure.

When I gave her a hug goodbye, I said, "I know there's something you're not telling me. I hope nothing has happened with you and Sandoval. I'm sorry for whatever you seem to be going through, but this shit has to stop. You can't spend as much time with him. He needs to focus on his relationship with Ariana." After what Raquel had said about Ariana threatening to take her own life if Tom broke things off, I was very concerned about her mental health. I felt like I needed to make sure she was okay first and foremost. But, in my head, I was also thinking that Raquel was in love with the boyfriend of one of her closest friends, and he was also one of her closest friends, and she knew she could never have him. Or maybe that was what I chose to believe.

When I got in my car and called Jenny, she said, "I think you might be right. She's definitely hiding something." And my gut instinct kicked in. I replied, "Right? Whether anything has happened or not, I don't know, but I feel like it could. What should I do?" Jenny suggested that I talk to Ariana. I knew she was correct, though I really didn't want to hurt Ariana unnecessarily, especially because she was already fielding the same suspicions from other people, and I was concerned about her mental health.

When I got home that night, Brock and I went in our hot tub, and I told him what was going on. He raised his voice, which I didn't appreciate since we lived in a condominium complex, and said, "Why the fuck would you think that about two of your best friends? That's not Raquel's or Tom's character." Since Tom had been my friend for years and we'd spent so much time with Raquel, Brock knew the two of them pretty well. He couldn't imagine them hurting Ariana, whom he also loved, like that.

To Brock, Sandoval was my number one guy friend, not just in the group but outside of the show. Prior to Brock, he'd been my person for many years. He'd even given me a few thousand dollars during the pandemic when I had no income, my podcast had been canceled, and I was pregnant. He was there for me when no one else was. Brock couldn't understand why I'd buy into such a horrible idea about my best friend (Tom) and my "little sister" (Raquel).

I said, "It's just that I've got Lala and Katie in my ear." And he replied, "Fuck Lala and Katie, you know Tom and Raquel better than they do. Tom and Raquel wouldn't do that to

Ariana." Brock totally changed my perspective, and I actually felt badly about assuming the worst. But I couldn't shake the feeling in my gut.

So, the following week, I reached out to Ariana, to see if she wanted to grab lunch. She'd either been busy or avoiding me through January. So, on February 1, we met at this cute Italian restaurant, Bottega Louie, in downtown LA. When we sat down, I said, "I need to ask you something. Please don't get upset with me, but—as your best friend—it's been on my mind, and I want to know what you're feeling." She said, "Sure, ask me anything." I took a deep breath and continued, "Do you think anything physical is going on with Tom and Raquel? Lala and Katie seem to." Ariana rolled her eyes and responded, "Oh my God, these fucking girls won't stay out of my relationship. No, I don't think anything's going on; you can trust me, Scheana. If Tom was going to cheat on me, Raquel would be the last person. They would never do that to me." I nodded and went on, "I had dinner with Raquel recently and she said that Tom confides things in her about your relationship. I just want to check how your mental health is doing." Ariana said, "Honestly, Scheana, I'm doing so much better. Things are good. Tom and I are having sex, and I'm in a really good place."

I have no idea if Ariana was being up-front with me, but she was very convincing in that moment, so I took her word for it, though I still couldn't completely let it go. Something wasn't sitting right with me.

Later that day, I was recording a podcast in the Valley with my friend Kael, who was also friends with Raquel and a very intuitive human. I invited Raquel to come watch the podcast and told Kael my doubts about her and Tom. After we wrapped the podcast, Raquel and I went outside to smoke a joint and talk some tea. With Kael within earshot, I revisited the conversation about Sandoval with Raquel, and again she denied, denied, denied. She even maintained that she'd heard what I said at dinner with Jenny and was pulling back on her friendship with Sandoval. I told her I was relieved, because I'd had lunch with Ariana earlier in the day, and she'd been resolute in the fact that she and Tom were great.

That night, I went out for drinks with Kael and Raquel. Kael was putting Raquel's feet to the fire about Sandoval, while we were texting from across the table that she wasn't being forthcoming. He was asking her a lot of questions about the nature of her relationship with Tom and also why she'd stopped sharing her location with us. This triggered a memory for me, from the week prior: After we were out one night, I'd texted Raquel to make sure she got home safely. When she didn't answer, I checked her location, and it wasn't loading. She then responded to me a minute later saying that her parking garage didn't have service, so I didn't think anything of it. Yet now it was bugging me. I said, "I need to ask you something. And I'm sorry to keep doing this, but why is your location turned off on your phone?" She said, "Oh, I just prefer it that way." I replied, "I don't think so. I've had your location for a year and a half and suddenly it's not available. I think you're hiding something; what is it?" Again, she said it was just a personal decision, and she texted as soon as she got home after our drinks.

Raquel even went one step further and texted me the following week, when she was out without me, to say that she was home safe. I recall thinking, hmm, I do appreciate it, but if your hands are clean, then turn your location back on.

Obviously, I now know that her location was off because she'd gone various places with Tom—from Big Bear and St. Louis to Chicago and Northern California.

At this point, I was almost positive that Raquel was lying, so I decided to take another approach and discuss it with Sandoval directly. Until this point, I'd held back on contacting him about it because I didn't want to insult him if I was totally wrong. I don't know why I kept pursuing it like a dog with a bone, mainly because if they'd been honest with me, I would have had to tell Ariana, and that was the last position I wanted to be in. Yet, clearly, I couldn't help myself.

That Sunday, February 5, a bunch of us were at TomTom for the launch of Ariana's Drink From Home Cloudberry cocktail. Sandoval went outside to smoke a cigarette by himself, and I took Brock's joint and followed Tom into the back alley. It seemed like as organic a moment as I'd ever have to talk to him without coming off as overly confrontational. Once we were standing face-to-face, I said to him, "Is there anything going on with you and Raquel?" Offended, he replied, "Why the fuck would you ask me that?" I said, "I think she has feelings for you." And he responded, "That's ridiculous; she's like a little sister to me." He then said, as Raquel had, that nothing had ever happened between them. He seemed so hurt, and I felt sure he wouldn't lie to me, so I completely bought it. It's actually shocking to realize just how duplicitous they were and how gullible I was. Tom and I hugged it out and I went back to the party to tell Brock he was right. Even though he wasn't.

A few weeks later, while I was in New York with Raquel doing press for *VPR*, the shit finally hit the fan.

The night we arrived, we went out to dinner with my friend

Nema, a former cast member from *Shahs of Sunset*. Raquel and Nema had casually dated the year prior, so he knew her pretty well. Immediately, he said to Raquel, "Your energy is off. I've never seen you like this." He wouldn't let it go, and I could tell Raquel was squirming, so I said, "Stop making her feel badly. She's been smoking weed and drinking; she's probably in another world." He agreed in the moment, but when Raquel got up to go to the bathroom, he doubled down that he felt she was hiding something. (I mean, join the club, dude.)

Little did we know that right before that dinner, Raquel had engaged in a very intimate FaceTime call with Sandoval (a conversation that was later uncovered by Ariana on Tom's phone).

The next morning, Raquel and I set out for a full press day with outlets such as *Us Weekly*, *New York Live*, *Page Six*, and Barstool Sports' *Chicks in the Office*. As we were doing the interviews, I noticed that Raquel was uncomfortable with some of the questions. When she was asked something, she'd direct her answer to me and avoid eye contact with the host. I could tell she was overwhelmed by the whole process. Up until that point Raquel had only done interviews, aside from her pageants, with James by her side. He answered all of the questions, and then she would occasionally chime in. This was the first time she was on her own, whereas I was seasoned and media trained, so I let her lean on me.

On the way to *Chicks in the Office*, which was our final stop before *Watch What Happens Live*, she said, "Can we please not do any more interviews?" I replied, "No, *Chicks in the Office* is at Barstool Sports and it's one of my favorite podcasts I've ever done." I reached for her hand, interlocked my fingers with hers, and added, "I've got your back. I will complete your sentences if I have to. After this, we only have *Watch What Happens Live*, which will be so fun." She relented and thanked me.

That night, on *Watch What Happens Live*, we played a little game where Andy asked us a bunch of questions, one of which was: Which Tom is hotter, Sandoval or Schwartz? Raquel and I got a point for every question we answered the same way. I was positive Raquel was going to say Schwartz because of the whole story line with her at my wedding. I genuinely think Schwartz is the better looking of the Toms, but I also knew that Sandoval's feelings would be hurt if we both said Schwartz. So I figured we wouldn't get a point for that one. But, when Andy said, one, two, three, Raquel blurted Sandoval, too. I had a huge reaction on live TV, as it was so unexpected. And, when we went to a commercial break, even Andy said he was confused. Raquel just shrugged and maintained, "Sandoval has better abs," which was true. Schwartz had more of a dad body.

Once we'd wrapped *WWHL*, we went to a bar called Brass Monkey on Little West Twelfth Street with some of my friends and some people who worked at Bravo. We downed a few drinks, but as they were closing the bar and turning off the lights, we couldn't find Raquel. Someone said she was in the bathroom, so we went outside to wait for her. That was when Raquel, who was clearly intoxicated, came out of the bar with Ariana on speakerphone. All I could hear was Ariana crying on the phone, and I thought, Oh shit, this is not good. Immediately, I got tunnel vision with the sole purpose of protecting Ariana. I told my friends to take the Bravo people somewhere else and we'd meet them there. I wanted to figure out what was wrong before anyone from the network got wind of it.

I said to Raquel, "What is going on?" She looked at me

blankly and confessed, "Tom Sandoval and I have been having an affair for seven months. Ariana just found out."

My jaw dropped open, and I completely lost it. Fury rose in my chest. I knew she was a fucking liar. I snatched her phone out of her hand and said, "Ariana, it's Scheana. I'm so sorry. I didn't want this to be true." I was sobbing, she was sobbing. Raquel was just standing there like lost Bambi with her eyes wide open, if Bambi had stolen his closest friend's boyfriend. I heard Tom screaming at Ariana in the background and, on instinct, I hurled Raquel's phone as far and hard as I could into a gutter in the street.

It was so surreal and kind of eerie. There we were at 2 a.m. in the middle of New York City without a single person or car in sight. I then marched over to Raquel, got in her face, and screamed, "How could you do this?" All she could say was, "I'm sorry," pitifully, before grabbing my wrist so I couldn't walk away. She wanted me to listen to her, but instead I pushed her off me. She came back toward me, so I shoved her again. This time, she stumbled into the wall of the building behind her. I yelled, "I cannot believe how disgusting you are," and I left her there.

Once I'd returned to the hotel, I called Ariana and said, "I pushed that bitch and threw her phone in the street." Ariana had me on speakerphone and Tom could hear from the background. Apparently, he thought I said, I punched that bitch. I'll admit there were a lot of emotions that night, but I did not punch Raquel.

The amusing thing is that one of my friends overheard Raquel, from the hallway, in her room talking to someone about the night, saying that I'd reacted reasonably. And that she wasn't upset with me. She said she deserved it. Agreed!

But her story changed after speaking to Sandoval. My guess is that Tom said something like "I heard Scheana punched you. Are you okay?" And then Raquel took that and ran with it, partly because she was questioning what actually happened, since she was too intoxicated to remember, and also because it seemed like she was being encouraged to reclaim the narrative by becoming the victim.

When we got back to LA, Ariana told production everything. She refused to protect Tom and Raquel. Why should she? They'd betrayed her in the worst possible way.

As soon as that happened, word slowly started circulating around the cast.

And, just like that, Scandoval exploded.

15

NOTES ON A SCANDAL

Once the Tom-Raquel-Ariana love triangle had made headlines around the world, I got a call from one of our producers, Jeremiah, who told me that the *VPR* cameras were going back up for season ten to chronicle the fallout from Scandoval.

This was not going to be the same as when they'd picked up cameras for a couple of days to capture my divorce from Shay. Oh no. Now, we were going to be filming for two full weeks and then still have a reunion, which they'd never done before. I was still on the day rate, so I was thinking: Put me in, coach! I ended up making more for the Scandoval episode than every other cast member, and I had hoped this would prove how valuable I was to the group—and the show—ahead of discussions for season eleven. But my only concern at that moment in time was making sure that Ariana felt loved, protected, and supported.

At this point, given how things had ended with me and Raquel and the narrative she was sharing about the heated exchange in New York City, a friend questioned how far Raquel might take her accusations. Would she escalate it beyond our mutual friends and *VPR* producers? Though I didn't punch or hit her, I did toss her phone and push her away from me, twice. So, being someone who has always been scared of getting in trouble, someone who instinctively taps the brakes when they see a police car, even when they aren't speeding, I asked this friend to call Raquel to find out what she was planning to do.

She told them there was no way she'd ever file charges or pursue this further, which I was very relieved to hear. However, this conversation must have occurred before she took her first meeting with a crisis PR agency, when it seemed to me that she decided to try to salvage her reputation amid the brewing scandal and shift the narrative from that of a femme fatale stealing her best friend's man to a Bambi-eyed victim.

It seemed to me that the first part of this reputational rehab was to highlight that Tom recorded an intimate FaceTime with Raquel without her consent, which resulted in the entire cast of *VPR* receiving cease-and-desist letters to their personal email accounts, inspiring Lala's famous and profitable "Send It to Darrell" merch line. On an embarrassing note, the lawyer who had sent those correspondences out to the cast, knowing full well that they all had legal representation and it wouldn't be appropriate to send to talent directly, was my long-time entertainment attorney, who I had set Raquel up with the year prior; he had helped her negotiate a sizable pay increase for season ten. Needless to say, I now have a new lawyer.

After that, Raquel filed a restraining order against me for our altercation in New York. To do so, she first needed to file a police report (which she filed in LA five days later, not in NYC, where our exchange occurred), have a doctor document her alleged injuries (so severe that they didn't require medical attention until four days later), and attest to the facts of the matter under penalty of perjury. This girl was willing to lie about me, put my livelihood and reputation in jeopardy, as well as expose herself to serious legal issues for filing a false report, just so that the media would go easier on her.

I can empathize with someone who falls for the wrong person and creates chaos in their personal life. Sometimes the heart wants what it shouldn't. But I will never understand how she could weaponize the justice system in such an irresponsible way, especially against someone who treated her as family, just to shield herself from the repercussions of her own poor decisions.

So, imagine my surprise when I was sitting at home alone with Summer, and my publicist called to inform me that TMZ was going to run a story that Raquel had filed to obtain a restraining order against me. Apparently, she was claiming that I'd assaulted her, resulting in a black eye and a "permanent scar" on her eyebrow.

Immediately I started freaking out and crying. Summer felt my fear and pain and teared up as well. The second I realized how scared she was, I knew I needed to reel it in and keep my shit together for her sake. Still, I was completely shocked and appalled. I felt sick to my stomach at the mere thought of how someone I'd allowed into my innermost circle could be capable of such deep levels of duplicity—not just the affair, but the subsequent lies to cover it up. And my OCD went into full swing. All I could do was agonize about the worst-case scenarios. Could I get arrested for an assault I didn't commit? Would I be fired from my job and lose necessary income? Might sponsors and brands back out of my podcast? Would I be canceled altogether? My intrusive thoughts were spinning out of control.

That same night, Ariana had some friends flying in from New York. They were all heading to Mexico the following day for a college friend's wedding, where she ultimately met her current boyfriend, Daniel Wai, so LA was just a stopover. Since I knew them, she asked if she could meet them at my house in Marina del Rey in order to escape the paparazzi who—at this time—were camped outside of Ariana and Tom's place around the clock. I said, "Of course. We'll go to Venice Beach at sunset." I thought that would be a nice break for Ariana amid all the craziness in her life.

Unfortunately, as they were driving to my house, Ariana noticed that the paparazzi were following her, which she immediately let me know. I didn't want the paparazzi to know where I lived or be anywhere near Summer, so I suggested that we meet at a nearby Mexican restaurant instead. Of course, that didn't throw them off our scent. The paparazzi were camped outside the window shooting photos of us inside the restaurant, which had me in a panic. It felt like such an invasion of privacy. As a mom, I felt extra protective of the little Marina bubble we were raising our daughter in. I had already given the media so much and just wanted to maintain this place for myself and my family, especially to keep Summer safe.

Thankfully, Summer and I were able to slip out through the kitchen and then the back door, and into the alley behind the restaurant, while everyone else used the front door. I carried Summer the whole way and tried to make it like an adventure for her. I said, "We're just walking a different route home. It'll be fun." I tried to act relaxed, but I was actually jogging, for fear that the paparazzi would figure out what we'd done and chase us back to my house.

Finally, I reconnected with Ariana and her friends on a street corner, and we returned to my complex safely, where we hung out for the rest of the night. Still, as grateful as I was to be sheltered and safely away from the prying eyes of those cameras, I broke down in tears. And my empathetic daughter was looking at me with such a sad face that my heart was breaking. Yes, I understood that the infidelity had happened to Ariana, not to me, but being stalked by paparazzi when you're with your child is extremely unnerving, especially for a person who is already struggling with anxiety. Not to mention that I was shaken by Raquel's false accusations, so I already felt like I was under attack.

I had to hire a lawyer for an as-yet-to-be-determined court date. I couldn't believe that it had come to that, and I started having full-blown panic attacks every single day. I'd never been in trouble with the law for anything, aside from a speeding ticket, so to potentially have assault charges or a restraining order on my record was horrifying. Was Raquel really afraid of me? Did she think I was going to lurk outside of her house or harass her? It was ridiculous, since all I actually wanted was to never see or speak to her again.

To make matters worse, Raquel's court filing included my

home address, so once the document hit the docket, my safe little bubble burst. The paparazzi started camping outside my house. I was terrified, to say the least. With every knock at the door and every stranger I encountered, I wondered if I was about to be served. I never was. It was obvious to me that this case was never about justice; it was about optics and headlines, and changing the media narrative. While living through that time was frightening, I'd be damned if that bitch was going to wrongly accuse me of something and get away with it.

My court date was set for Wednesday, March 29, 2023, six days following the scheduled season ten reunion taping on Thursday, March 23, though I wasn't even sure I'd be able to attend. The temporary restraining order (TRO) stipulated that I must stay one hundred yards away, and I figured the producers would prioritize Raquel being there to face the music for her seven-month affair with Tom Sandoval.

On March 17, the week prior to the taping, Raquel's attorney reached out to my attorney to see if we might be able to sort out a settlement agreement, which would include Raquel withdrawing her TRO, thus allowing us to both participate onstage together at the reunion. That should have been welcome news, right? I wanted to attend the reunion and put the whole nightmare behind me! But once my attorney reviewed the settlement agreement that Raquel's attorney had prepared, we had three notes:

1. *Raquel agreed to file a request to end the TRO and take off-calendar the hearing on the permanent restraining order.* Unfortunately, there is no mechanism to terminate a civil temporary restraining

order early, so it would have to lapse on March 29, six days after the reunion taping.

2. *Raquel agreed she would not participate in the prosecution of any claims or allegations as set forth in the police report that she filed.* This wouldn't be sufficient because Raquel would have to appear pursuant to a subpoena if the district attorney or city attorney filed charges. We would need a declaration from Raquel that I did not punch her and that the push was reasonable force in response to Raquel grabbing my wrist. We agreed that if Raquel provided such declaration, we would not release it and would use it only if the district or city attorney threatened to file charges.

3. *They requested that both of us issue a mutually agreed upon joint statement.* On this one, I just had no interest in signing my name to a shared statement with her.

Raquel's attorney did not respond to these comments. Instead, they went to the press. On March 29, ETOnline.com reported that "prior to the reunion and behind the scenes, Leviss' and Shay's teams tried to work out an agreement so the two could film the reunion together, but it fell apart."

The outlet further quoted an unnamed source, which in situations like this is often a publicist who wants their comments to read more like insider tea than a rep statement, saying, "Raquel's team, with production's knowledge, attempted to find a mutually acceptable resolution with Scheana to help get the TRO dropped prior to filming so that they could both attend the reunion together. Raquel's team proposed they would both agree that the argument escalated and got physical but that both women wished to move forward from it, agreed there was no fault, would stop talking about it after the reunion, and would stop making any disparaging remarks related to the incident after the reunion. Had they come to a reasonable agreement Raquel was prepared to appear in court Tuesday [note: the hearing date was actually on a Wednesday] to drop the TRO. Unfortunately, Scheana rebuked the offer, which kept the burden on production to find a solution for them to film separately…Scheana's team wanted Raquel to say the punch never happened, and Raquel refused."

This was deeply frustrating and a misrepresentation of the events that had occurred, since my team never "rebuked" her offer but instead raised legitimate concerns and was met with silence, one of which was that the settlement wouldn't unburden production. And if I were guilty of what Raquel had alleged in her police report and court filings, I would not have been in a position to turn down a settlement offer.

Up until the day before the reunion, I still wasn't sure if I'd be able to attend. I certainly wasn't going to risk the repercussions of violating the terms of the TRO, even if that meant missing out on a sizable paycheck. Thankfully, production ended up finding a solution, ensuring that Raquel and I would never be within one hundred yards of each other. A trailer was set up off-site, equipped with a live feed and several cameras to capture every reaction. I started out onstage with the rest of the cast and Andy Cohen, while Raquel was in the trailer. Then, in the afternoon, when it was time to bring Raquel to the stage, the carefully orchestrated swap began. Raquel and I were each placed in cars at the same time and sent in different directions. It felt like I had driven several miles away from the studio. However, when I exited the car to enter the trailer, I realized that I ended up in a parking lot across the street from the studio where the reunion was being filmed.

While onstage during the first part of the reunion, with Raquel watching from the trailer, Andy Cohen handed me a piece of paper, which he stated was a court filing showing that Raquel was dropping the restraining order against me. This should have made me happy, but I knew something was amiss. It couldn't be that easy. I sent my lawyer a screenshot of the document, and we debriefed once I was settled in the trailer. I don't believe this footage has seen the light of day, but after he explained to me that the document had no legal significance, and was essentially worthless, I ripped it up right there on camera. Since no one can terminate a civil temporary restraining order prior to the court hearing and the court hadn't even processed the document, it was obvious that this was a stunt purely for the TV cameras, not an action that had any merit in the courtroom.

Why would she do this if it didn't mean anything? Well, as mentioned, the reunion was taped the week prior to our court date. My team and I were very confident that the facts were on our side, and our sense was that Raquel's team concurred with our assessment, even though they were saying the opposite to the news media. I can only speculate, but I imagine that they were worried that when the case would be dismissed, the media coverage would lean more favorably to me, less so for Raquel. To prevent that from happening and to maintain control of the media narrative, Raquel came out with a statement prior to the court date where she essentially said that she was taking "the high road" and dropping the TRO, before the facts could be heard in court.

Ironically, when I showed up with my attorney to my scheduled court hearing to hopefully put this nightmare behind me once and for all, Raquel and her team stated that *I* was the one being performative. Excuse me, when was I performing?

When the stress of this case whittled me below 110 pounds, a weight I hadn't seen on the scale since I'd battled anorexia during my early twenties?

When my empathetic daughter mimicked my cries?

When I sat outside a nail salon in the Valley waiting for a paparazzo to come find me so that I could candidly deliver a prepared statement? *Oh, that's right…*

There is nothing performative about clearing your name from false allegations, especially when I had to contend with the court of public opinion. I attended the hearing because the judge could have decided to enforce a permanent restraining order against me. Sure, Raquel stated that she wasn't going to show up to court so I didn't need to, either, but could I trust her? Would *you* trust her? I needed to put this behind me once and for all. Believe me, I would have much rather been home in bed with my kid that rare rainy morning in LA than driving to the Van Nuys courthouse. Raquel certainly got the luxury of staying dry and getting her beauty rest that day—from the comfort of Tom Sandoval and Ariana Madix's shared home, while Ariana was out of town for work.

My relationship with Raquel was not the only one rocked by this scandal. During this ordeal and sometime earlier in the month, Sandoval—to whom I was not speaking at all—texted me to say he had some information for me and asked if I could call him later. Even though I was furious with him, I was curious to hear him out, so I agreed. Once I was on the line with Tom, I made sure Brock was in earshot, as a witness. Fool me once. Tom said, "I want to let you know that Raquel's family has her in a Britney Spears sort of situation, where she's not allowed to have her phone. She snuck a few calls to me from the bathroom, but—aside from that—they're not letting her speak to me. As far as I know, her parents have hired a private investigator to track down the footage from the street that night. So, Scheana, if you punched her, you can deny it all you want, but if they access the video and it shows otherwise, it's going to be very bad for you."

Honestly, I wanted there to be video footage, to prove that I'd never punched Raquel, but either they never uncovered the footage or they did and it confirmed my narrative of events, as it never materialized. Could that be the real reason Raquel decided to *dip out* on attending the court hearing?

I'd like to think that, in that moment, Tom was acting as the good friend that he'd been to me for fourteen years, giving me that heads-up because he was looking out for my well-being. However, since he was also this person who'd had an illicit affair with his girlfriend's close friend—the person now dragging my name through the mud—for seven months, I realized it could have been a threat rather than a heads-up. I wasn't sure I could trust him anymore, which was sad to come to terms with.

I told Tom that I'd already retained a lawyer and asked if I could put him in touch to get more details on the private investigator situation. While I knew I was innocent, I still wanted to stay on top of it. And Tom said yes.

There was a part of me that struggled with cutting Tom out of my life. He had been a solid friend to me for so long, and I wasn't one to just discard someone because they've made mistakes. I've made numerous mistakes myself. Naturally, my energy went to Ariana in this situation; she was the one who needed it. But did that mean I had to cut Tom out forever? There'd been a lot of incestuous infidelity within this friend group over the years, and we'd always been able to find our way through. With time, would we be able to navigate this as well? In the moment, a line was drawn in the sand, and my loyalty was to Ariana. Unfortunately, siding with Ariana didn't ultimately preserve our friendship.

In the months leading into season eleven, Ariana's star rose as the world rallied around her postscandal, and a little distance emerged in our friendship. She's not great at multitasking, and she was being pulled in a million different directions. Still, throughout this time, I was living in my own personal hell and I desperately wanted my best friend, my ride-or-die throughout ten seasons of *VPR* plus the two years prior serving up Big Pinkys at Villa Blanca together, to notice and ask what was wrong. She never did, and she still doesn't know that my world came to a screeching halt shortly after hers did, for more reasons than Raquel's restraining order. No matter how much distance has emerged, the love is always there. I will continue to support Ariana in everything she does and will always be cheering for her. She's an enormously talented person, and I'm so proud of her. When I saw her play Roxie Hart in *Chicago* on Broadway, I cried tears of joy. She was amazing. After seeing her at her lowest, I'm thrilled that she was able to turn such a dark period in her life into so much light and success.

Once we started filming season eleven, Lisa Vanderpump sat Lala and me down on camera to relay her concern for Tom's mental state, saying that he revealed he was struggling with suicidal thoughts. When I heard that, I knew that I would never forgive myself if something happened to him. Regardless of what he'd done, his crimes did not merit the death penalty. Does that mean I owe him my friendship? No, but I could show him some grace…the grace I wish I would have shown Collin all those years ago.

Had I known that extending Tom grace at that time would ultimately strain my relationship with Ariana, I don't know what I would have done differently. Sure, there's a chance Tom might have been playing us all with his mental health struggles, but I'll always take such claims seriously. Regardless, my friendship with Tom never recovered from Scandoval. If this wasn't cemented already, it was in July 2024, when I saw the news that he was suing Ariana for invasion of privacy after she had discovered the FaceTime recording of Raquel on his phone. I had hoped that Tom would grow from his mistakes and become a better man. I'd like to think that everyone has the potential to change for the better. However, that move showed he wasn't interested in bettering himself, just his self-interest. I simply couldn't get behind him suing Ariana and forcing any more trauma on her. I obviously knew he could go low, but this was a new depth for him. Tom did revoke his motion a couple of days later following the intense public backlash; though, of course, he took no accountability and blamed it on his lawyer. It's always someone else's fault.

I actually saw Tom and his new girlfriend recently at the Vanderpump Dog Foundation Gala, and we said a quick hello. I can be cordial. There doesn't need to be more drama with Tom.

On that same evening, I realized that my relationship with Lisa Vanderpump had diminished, too. Earlier in the year, back in January 2024 at the Creative Arts Emmy Awards, held at the Microsoft Theater in downtown LA, Lisa completely snubbed me in the lobby, while everyone was congregated. When I saw her, I said, "Our dresses really complement each other's," because we both had black feather detailing, and I suggested we get a photo together. Lisa started to get in position, then had a moment of realization and said, "Actually, no. Why don't you ask Kyle Richards for another photo? I saw you posted one with her the other day."

The photo in question was from Kathy Hilton's Christmas Party the previous month. I was totally caught off guard, mainly because after ten seasons of not being nominated, we finally were, and I was so proud of what we'd accomplished. It's a shame to let something so petty cloud such a special moment. I replied, "Wait, are you being serious? You're not going to take a selfie with me?" And she said, "No," and then walked away. Though a month later, at the season eleven premiere event for *VPR*, Lisa had no problem crashing my photo with the girls from the cast. I said to her, "Oh, *now* you want a photo with me." To which she responded, "Where's your best friend Kyle Richards?" I joked, "Oh, I'm meeting up with her after this." Lisa fired back, "Of course you are," before turning her attention to photographers and striking a pose.

Fast-forward to that night at the Vanderpump Dog Foundation Gala, which Pandora had pleaded with me to attend. Lisa was downright cold. She posed for snapshots with Stassi, but—even when we were standing next to each other on the carpet—she wouldn't be in a photo with me. The brief communication we had involved her berating me for why Lala hadn't attended, to which I responded, "Well, I'm here."

She snarled back, "As you should be." All those years that I'd been her good little solider, apparently one photo with her nemesis was all it took to unravel me into an enemy.

The upheaval to my inner circle during this period in my life shook me to my core. Unfortunately, the worst was yet to come.

16

THE WHOLE TRUTH

n the throes of Scandoval and its aftermath, my own world shattered. Since Raquel had doxed my address when she filed the restraining order, my only safe place no longer felt secure. Every day, I was gritting my teeth and trying to power through this mess, not really knowing what my life would look like on the other side of it.

By the end of March, once we'd filmed the reunion and the restraining order had been dismissed, I assumed my life would settle down. Silly me. The story of the scandal was far from done, and it became clear that the media was going to have a field day with it for quite some time to come. Each morning, I would wake up to a new headline or viral video while attempting to parent an almost two-year-old who had no idea what was going on. I knew I had to stay strong for her, but it was one of the most stressful and uncertain periods of my entire life.

That was when blind items about Brock and Raquel having an affair surfaced. Prior to Tom and Raquel's indiscretions, Brock had been supportive of Raquel when she split from James. Even though I knew in my heart that the gossip concerning Brock and Raquel was ridiculously fake, we had to deal with it anyway. There was the smallest section of my brain that kept thinking: If Tom and Raquel pulled the wool over everyone's eyes for seven months, could Brock and Raquel have done the same thing? When such a monumental lie is exposed so close to you, it brings a lot into question.

That wasn't the only blind item about Brock and another woman to emerge during this time. There was also one about him dating a woman in San Diego around the same time we met, which claimed that Brock would spend Saturdays with her, before coming up to see me on Sundays for Chargers games. It also alleged that she had helped him pack for the Australia trip where we made our relationship official, prompting her to cut ties with him. I certainly didn't trust Raquel as far as I could throw her, so when Brock dismissed the accusations and denied that some woman helped him pack, I believed him.

Miraculously, by Easter—between filming seasons ten and eleven—media attention and fan speculation had died down a little, and paparazzi were no longer camped outside my house. We had an amazing day with my family, and that night Brock and I sat down to watch the latest episode of *The Real Housewives of New Jersey.* It was a typical evening at home for us, and—finally—my nervous system wasn't firing on all cylinders. I guess I should have known better than to relax into my state of calmness.

Right before I pressed play, Brock told me to put down the remote because he needed to talk to me about something important. I thought he was joking at first. But then I noticed his face was serious, and my heart began beating against my chest. What else could possibly go wrong? Brock said that with all of the fake news being published, he was afraid that something that actually *was* true might surface, and it was best that I heard it directly from him.

My whole body froze, and I remained in a state of paralyzed shock as he confessed that he'd cheated on me two years prior, when we were living in San Diego during the pandemic, while I was pregnant with Summer. I had spent so much time fighting off my anxiety and convincing myself that just because Tom cheated on Ariana didn't mean Brock would ever cheat on me. Now, I was finding out just how wrong I was.

As I sat there, feeling completely sick to my stomach, he admitted that—at the time—he was scared about being a father again, specifically about whether he even deserved to be, and he chose to deal with it by sleeping with someone else. I use the word "chose" because it was very much a conscious decision. No one twisted his arm or dragged him into bed.

Just when I thought my world had been rocked beyond anything I could have imagined, it was officially shattered into pieces—pieces I wasn't sure I could put back together. I didn't want to believe what he was telling me, and, oddly, I didn't know how to react, either. I was so angry, so sad, and so hurt; those were givens. There was this deep fury bubbling inside of me, and I couldn't release it. If I screamed, I could wake up my daughter. *Our* daughter. *His* baby, whom I'd been carrying while he was in bed with another woman. I stood up and started pacing back and forth, fuming, and feeling like I might throw up.

Then, unable to contain my rage, I slapped him and threw a Rubik's cube in his direction, which he dodged. To this day, every time I see a Rubik's cube it triggers me, pulling me right back to this incredibly dark moment in my life. Same goes for any mention of an F45 gym.

Brock didn't know what to say. What could he possibly say? He'd done what he'd done, and it wasn't going to go away or be swept under the rug. Still, I wanted details. I had to know who the woman was and why he'd so blatantly betrayed me, particularly during such a vulnerable period of my life.

He said that the woman was someone he had known since before we met. One day, while I was at home, pregnant with his child, Brock went to work at his gym, F45 Training East Hillcrest in San Diego, and he ran into her outside. After reconnecting, he said they began a brief affair. I was a little confused because I'd always had his location and could have checked it at any time. How had I not caught them? But he also had a second phone for work, which I did know about but didn't monitor. It turned out that was their sole form of communication. Nice, right?

That same night, Brock gave me a letter that he'd written a year after the affair ended. Why then? I wondered. Apparently, he had compartmentalized his indiscretion (convenient, I know), but while we were out at a local festival in San Diego one night, he ran into some old friends who reminded him of that time in his life, and everything that he'd done came rushing back. He said he realized he was throwing his second chance at a family away by stepping out and swore to himself that he would never betray me again.

That night after the festival, he wrote the letter, which included more specifics than I ever wanted, such as how many times they'd slept together, where they'd done it, and where they hadn't (our house). He also pointed out that it was purely physical, never emotional, and he always used protection. *Gee, thanks!* He definitely wasn't sober when he put pen to paper, so the spelling errors were rampant. I can't explain why, but that really irritated me. Maybe because it felt like another sign of his carelessness. Once I'd read it, that was more than enough. I told him to immediately toss it into the fire. I never wanted to set eyes on those words again.

Then I texted his sister, whom I'm very close with, to call me. After I filled her in, she scolded Brock, while asking how she could support me, our relationship, and our family unit. I didn't know what I wanted or needed in that moment, but she also instructed Brock to be tender with me.

The letter made me remember the weeks leading up to my second trimester when, like many pregnant women, I was sexually stimulated. I'll never forget how, during that time, Brock was "afraid" to have sex with me (or he simply didn't want to). That did a number on my anxiety, and it killed my confidence in a way I can't even describe. His behavior now made so much more sense.

The following day, as soon as I'd stopped crying for more than a few seconds at a time, I called my publicist and told him what had happened. I said I needed him on high alert in case something came out in the press. Then, instead of wallowing in bed like I wanted to, I put on a brave face—literally. I had an eyelash extension appointment, and I decided not to cancel it. When you have your lashes done, you can't get them wet for forty-eight hours, which worked out well. I had to be on *E! News* that night and had a business dinner that Brock was supposed to come to with me, but I lied and said he had to stay home with Summer. I also told my mom we didn't need her help with babysitting, because I knew I couldn't face her, nor could I tell her until I'd made sense of everything myself.

For the next few nights, Brock slept in the spare bedroom. There was a part of me that wanted to be close to him, since I was used to him being the one to comfort me, but I also couldn't stand the thought of him touching me. Honestly, I didn't know what I wanted other than for none of it to be true. It felt like everyone around me was deceiving me or letting me down. And the one person I thought I could lean on during all of it had betrayed me first. I have never felt so alone, and throughout it all I had to act happy and normal in front of Summer.

Five days later, I went to Coachella with Brock, Ariana, and some other friends. The last thing I wanted to do was attend a music festival with my unfaithful husband, but I had two contracted brand deals that I couldn't get out of easily. What would my excuse be—to the brands as well as to Ariana and the rest of the group? I was also looking forward to meeting Dan, Ariana's new boyfriend, that weekend. Of course, Brock and I had photos taken of us at one of the gifting tents, and looking back at those pics, we appeared completely happy and normal, as if my whole world wasn't crumbling. Faking normalcy in front of our friends felt nearly impossible. I didn't want to bring the mood down, especially around Ariana, who seemed to be happy and blissful for the first time in a while.

People have said I was jealous of Ariana because she was on *Dancing with the Stars* and had all these amazing opportunities presented to her. But the only time during the Scandoval saga that I even got close to a feeling of envy for Ariana was related to the fact that she got to put Tom's affair behind her without a legal union to dissolve or child to consider. While I never wanted to compare traumas, and our circumstances were different, I did resent that it couldn't be so clean-cut for me. And as much as I wanted to put Brock on blast and feel supported during that dark time, this was Summer's father—not just my husband.

On night two of the festival I was in full brokenhearted emo mode, and some of my friends seemed to sense it, Dayna being the main one. As I sat with her on the grass, watching I don't even remember who, she let me lean back on her and then gently kissed me, which turned into a short, sensual make-out right in front of Brock's face. He knew how broken I was because of what he'd done, and I knew how much it crushed him to see me kiss another woman. When I got up to go to the bathroom he said to me, "Please don't *ever* do that again," to which I responded, "Doesn't feel good, does it?" I was, again, Scheana in revenge mode wanting to hurt the man who'd betrayed me. But this time it was different. It was bigger than just me and my feelings. An eye for an eye wouldn't work anymore as trying to get back at my husband also meant hurting my daughter and further disrupting the world we had created as a family. Even if our marriage wasn't going to ultimately survive this hurdle, I knew I couldn't complicate things further, nor make the situation any messier than it already was.

The week after Coachella, I was set to appear on *WWHL*. The network called and asked if Brock could be the guest alongside of me since he wasn't featured as much in our wedding season, and they wanted to throw him a bone. Normally I would have been thrilled to sit next to my man on my favorite late-night talk show, but this time it was a hard pass. I explained that we both couldn't leave Summer again after Coachella so I would be coming solo. (They ended up booking Michael Rapaport as the guest instead, which couldn't have been more fun! It was the confidence boost I needed while feeling at my lowest.) Brock and I left Coachella on day three, and nobody questioned it since they knew I had to fly cross-country. I couldn't fake it one more day, and I missed Summer terribly.

As soon as I dropped my bags in NYC, I went to meet Nema for dinner. He was one of the only people in the world whom I trusted 100 percent, and I needed to tell one other person about what I was going through. Someone who wasn't related to Brock or on my payroll. He was the comfort I desired in that moment, and I'll forever be grateful to him for being there for me in my most vulnerable and depressed state. We had dinner, went back to my hotel, and he just let me vent and sob with zero judgment while also telling me he supported whatever decision I made for my family.

Months passed and I continued to struggle in silence. I felt like I needed to practice self-care and be the best version of myself for my daughter; that was my main concern. There was a moment when Brock hugged me, and Summer wanted to get in on it because she loves a group hug. She put her arms around both of our necks, pulled us together, and said, "We're a family." That made me sad, and a bit resentful, but also hopeful that I'd find a way to keep our little unit of three together. I didn't want Summer to grow up in a split household. But I wasn't there yet.

I've thought about whether I would have married Brock if I'd known about the affair prior. Probably not. And Brock knew that. I do believe that he's been faithful to me ever since, but I'll always wonder. When he says he's going for a run, doesn't want to take his phone, and forgets his Apple Watch, is he really out exercising? I pray one day I'll be able to stop these intrusive thoughts and questions.

Before anyone knew, I recall sitting at Janet's baby shower and listening to her, Lala, and others talk about how they'd never stay with their man if they knew they'd been cheated on and that it takes a really strong bitch to stay. They then turned to me and our friend Michelle and said, "You guys agree, right?"

In that moment I saw Michelle's expression shift and noticed that she was uncomfortable with the question, as if she'd remained with her significant other, Jesse, after he'd cheated. I wanted to ask her about it then and there, but it wasn't the time or the place. Instead, I chimed in and said, "I don't know what I'd do. I've always said I would leave, too, but depending on the situation, especially after you start a family, it changes things." Pregnant Janet sat there, stared me dead in the face, and declared, "Nope, I'm out if that happens." I locked eyes with Michelle and gave her a look that communicated: I feel you, and your decision to stay (for now) is okay! Thank God she ended up leaving her toxic relationship.

For so long I wanted to open up to Janet and Lala about their sentiments that day and how I'll never forget them, but I couldn't.

To make matters worse, I still didn't know whom I could trust. I didn't tell people because of Summer and my desire to protect her. I knew whatever I revealed about her father would be out in the world forever. If I didn't have a child to think about, my reaction would have been very different. Also, I knew that once the cat was out of the bag, I couldn't put it back in. I desperately wanted support and to lean on those closest to me, but, at the same time, I wanted to protect my family and figure out what was best for all of us in the long run. I needed to sort out my feelings first and foremost. Two of my best friends had just been duplicitous in the worst way, one of whom put me in legal peril as part of her own PR strategy, and my husband had cheated on me. I'd been living in a house of lies for years. I had to get my bearings and not act impulsively. I worried that if I told my castmates, it would likely leak. And that if I chose to work through it with Brock, the world would hate him even more and then hate me for going back to him. It felt like a lose-lose situation, and I couldn't even talk to my closest friends about the best course of action.

A group of us went out to dinner at Chili's one night during a time while this was weighing heaviest on me. After returning home, sensing something was off with me, Lala texted and asked if I was okay. I wasn't, but I said that I was. Even though Lala didn't know what was going on, just feeling like someone was keeping tabs on me gave me some solace and helped me feel a little less alone. While Lala and I had become pretty close by that point in time, the history of our friendship has been tumultuous.

Among this friend group, Ariana had always been my person, my vault, the one who knew me so well that she could detect when something was off first—and vice versa. It surprised me that she never even noticed how stressed and sad I was. I feel like if she would've inquired, I would've opened up and trusted her. But I didn't want to burden her with my family problems as she was going through enough on her own. A part of me also worried that if I did choose to open up about it then, that it would come off as opportunistic, like I was crafting a publicity stunt to elicit the support and opportunities that Ariana was receiving.

The crazy thing is that, throughout season eleven, which we started filming at the end of June, it looked like I was constantly crying over Tom Sandoval. And, yes, it was extremely difficult to deal with my emotions toward him and reconcile them with the decade and a half of friendship we'd had before everything happened. But my main source of devastation—which barely anyone knew about—was due to Brock's infidelity. In some ways, it all felt like karma for what I'd unknowingly done to Brandi all those years ago. Mostly, it felt like a waking nightmare.

About five months after Brock confessed to me, I ran into a friend in Vegas who did not know about Brock's affair, nor did I tell her. She revealed that her baby's father had been unfaithful to her. She emphasized the importance of forgiveness and said she tried everything to keep their family together (unfortunately, it wasn't in the cards for them). She also made me promise to do the same no matter what happened between me and Brock. I want to be clear that this isn't the reason I stayed, though, initially, it did help me see things from a different angle. And it was what I needed to hear in that moment to feel okay with my decision not to leave.

When push came to shove, I had a choice to make. Option A: I could give up on Brock and our family, but I would be throwing our life away, fracturing my family, and hanging on to the hatred that was eating me alive. Or Option B: I could choose to forgive. I could begin to let go of the animosity and resentment and keep moving forward.

I chose Option B. After forgiving my own husband, I felt I had to forgive Tom Sandoval, too. When I told Ariana I couldn't keep hating Tom for her, this was why. Because then I would have had to continue despising my husband as well. I couldn't make sense of releasing one but not the other. I had to liberate the demons inside of me, if I was going to be the parent Summer needed and the person I wanted to be.

Even now, I haven't fully healed, but Brock and I have done a lot of work since then. He and I are both in therapy, and EMDR has been such a big part of reprogramming my brain to deal with this trauma stacked on top of more trauma. Maybe putting the truth on paper for the world to read and still standing by my husband is also part of the healing process. I never wanted to admit it to anyone, mainly because I didn't want to believe it was true or to have people think I was pathetic for staying, but I want to tell my full story, and this is an important part of it.

Unfortunately, my choice to reveal this secret on my own terms was compromised when one of the four people I'd told leaked it. Like most first-time authors, I was collaborating with a seasoned writer to help share my story. I thought the process would be fun and fulfilling. But, instead, it began with stress, tears, panic attacks, and a massive betrayal when I traveled to New York, in June 2024, for the *WWHL* fifteen-year anniversary party. During the same visit, I met with various publishing houses to try to sell my book.

One day after it sold, I found out that someone had—either unknowingly or knowingly—revealed Brock's affair to a gossip site. The blind item wasn't wholly accurate, but it was out there.

And I was terrified that it would spread like wildfire and destroy my family. Brock and I were almost back on solid ground, and I was worried public scrutiny would be too destabilizing. There were four possible culprits: Brock's sister, my publicist, my friend Nema, and the writer I was collaborating with. I couldn't fathom that Brock's sister, my publicist, or Nema would be disloyal, as I trusted them unconditionally, though I did have to ask, which was awkward and uncomfortable for all of us. After being lied to by so many of the people close to me, this process was super traumatizing as it made me further question my very inner circle of trust. I felt unbelievably paranoid.

When I decided I was going to hire a private investigator to look into the IP address that the blind item originated from and my lawyer sent a retroactive NDA with more comprehensive confidentiality language, my writer had a mental health crisis, quit, and soft-blocked me on Instagram. Nothing says "guilty" more than that!

While I wasn't happy about it, the leak did encourage me to come clean about Brock's transgression, and it forced him to confess to my mom and sister, whom I was most afraid to tell. This was a huge relief and much healthier for me than holding it in, as it's an important part of who I am today and who I've become in the last few years.

As I said, I'm still not mended from everything that happened, but rebuilding the trust and respect in our marriage is a project that Brock and I have both chosen to take on. We love each other so much, and we love our daughter. We've both made mistakes in our lives.

My plan was to open up about the affair on season twelve, as I needed time to process what had transpired and decide what I was going to do before facing the world. I was dying inside and broken, but not ready to divulge such a painful secret. The blind item forced my hand. Unfortunately, I won't get that chance with the show, so I'm doing it here and taking control of my narrative for the first time in a long time.

With that said, after eleven seasons on a show that, at its core, is about infidelity, I've come to believe that cheating doesn't always have to mean a relationship is over. For Tom and Ariana, it did. Sandoval destroyed their bond far beyond repair. But for me and my marriage, infidelity will always be a part of our story. It's just not going to be the way the story ends.

17

FIELD OF DREAMS

At this point in my life, I've got a lot more healing to do. I've endured betrayal by close friends, a divorce, a miscarriage, a traumatic birth, been both the other woman and the jilted woman. And I'm still battling OCD and navigating treatment every day.

As I said in the beginning, I've always been my own person and someone who forges her own path. But I've also been a people pleaser who's struggled to fit in at times, and this has been a constant challenge for me, one that I'm working to overcome.

In the wake of my divorce, I feel like I learned a number of essential lessons. The first was to keep my finances separate, which also meant asking Brock to sign a prenuptial agreement. While I didn't know about his affair when we got married, in retrospect, I'm glad I had the foresight to put that in place.

Unfortunately, as a result of my rocky history with men, I no longer believe in forever. Between Shay's addiction, his lies, and Brock's infidelity, I've become more wary than I probably need to be, but there's nothing I can do to change that. Trust requires time. And pain demands repair. I don't know how long it will take, but I do know that I'm going to do everything within my power to hold my family together. Right now, I'm trying to live by the mantra that my past doesn't have to define my future.

The fact is, marriage isn't easy. It's hard work, every single day. And Brock and I are two extremely different people. He was raised on a farm in New Zealand, the youngest of five kids. I was brought up as an only child for twelve-plus years, just outside of Los Angeles. Sometimes it seems like we have completely opposite outlooks on life—from his laid-back attitude toward everything and my overarching hyperfocus, to his relaxed approach as a dad and my helicopter parenting.

Another area where our opinions vary, and where I have more soul-searching to do, is whether or not to have another child. Both my miscarriage and Summer's traumatic birth continue to have a big impact on my psyche. I will never try to get pregnant again. I don't want to take that chance with my own life or my baby's life. It's not worth it to me. If we have the means and the frozen eggs to involve a surrogate one day, I'll consider that option. If Summer ends up being an only child—since she isn't growing up with her half siblings—I'm completely okay with that.

Though sometimes I worry Brock is not, and that if I don't give him another kid, one day, he may leave me for someone younger. It's an intrusive thought I don't actually believe, but they pop up. I'm five years older than he is, and I know he wants more children. For now, I'm not mentally there. I'm fine with having an eight-year age gap between Summer and a younger sibling; after all, my sister and I are twelve years apart and closer than ever. And Brock's priority right now is building a bridge to his other two children in Australia.

I think Brock has come to terms with understanding that we're putting a pause on the kid conversation. He also gets that the risk is too high for me to carry another baby, because he believes in science, and—according to my doctor—my body is likely not equipped to reach full term the natural way. The chances of miscarriage and HELLP syndrome are much higher now, and that risk is not one I'm willing to take. Nor am I willing to risk Summer growing up without a mother, just so I can try to give her a sibling. Why would I intentionally put myself through that kind of distress?

I'm not saying never to more kids, just not now. I'll admit that when I see Summer with my friends' babies, I think, Wow, she would be such a good big sister. I'd like to give her that opportunity in a few years. I also want to enjoy this special time with her, just the three of us, sometimes just the two of us, because I know once we have another child it will change the dynamics of our little family unit forever. I'm not prepared for that transformation yet. I want to be able to travel with my daughter and not have to worry about another baby whose diaper needs changing.

Summer is also a smart girl, which means I'll have to explain to her why I'm not the one who's pregnant if we adopt or use a surrogate. I'm afraid to be honest and say that I got really sick after I had her, because then she might think it was her fault that I can't have another baby. When she's older than four, I believe she'll be able to comprehend this more easily, without feeling as much distress.

I also have to consider the impact of my OCD, which will likely intensify with a second child in the picture. I already spend way too much energy worrying about Summer, and the feelings of fear and anxiety that are inherent in this disorder can often be triggered by things you least expect. This came into focus for me even more in 2023, when I was approached to produce and share my story in a documentary about being victimized by Juan Aponte at Hooters and becoming the face of a major lawsuit at age eighteen. I hadn't thought about that experience in twenty years, and when it resurfaced, I realized that I'd compartmentalized so much of what had happened to me. Suddenly, as a mom, it hit so differently and activated my OCD. I was already concerned about Summer choking or falling down, but, as soon as I had to revisit this past trauma and started thinking about Summer as a teenager and beyond, my obsessive tendencies kicked into an even higher gear.

As a kid, I was pretty strong and always powered through everything, namely being bullied. And, as a people pleaser with an independent constitution, I kept my mouth shut so as not to burden my loved ones. Now, I see that Summer is a carbon copy of me at that age—she's got a tough exterior but she's sensitive on the inside. I'm terrified that something bad will happen to her, and she'll hold it in the way I did. It's like watching myself grow up in real time.

Summer is such a little perfectionist, which isn't necessarily a good thing. I tell her all the time, it's okay to get dirty, it's okay to fall down, it's okay if you get paint on your clothing. As much as I love my mom, she raised me to be afraid of messiness and imperfection, even though I know she did the absolute best she could, at nineteen years old, with the tools she was given. I had an amazing childhood, and I wouldn't change a thing, because it's made me who I am today. I do, however, want to break the generational cycle and raise Summer in my own way.

I don't want Summer to develop OCD, although I know it's not something I can prevent, and it can be genetic. I want her to be courageous but cautious. I want to teach her right from wrong, yet have her learn how to recover when she stumbles. I'm not always going to be there to catch her, but I will always be here for her to talk to. I don't want her to be flawless. I want her to be her.

My urge to let her learn for herself is coming up a lot right now as she speaks more and more. Right now—at three and a half—Summer is adding an "ed" at the end of her past tense verbs. So, she'll say, "I lookeded at that." My mom corrected her the first time and suggested I do the same, to which I said no. Not only do I think it's adorable, but Summer isn't going to speak that way for the rest of her life. She's just working on understanding the past tense, which is part of the learning process. I'm sure, like every parent, I'm going to screw some things up, but I'm trying my best to not breed anxiety. Thankfully, Brock balances that out. He's not worried about ink poisoning when she colors on her hands, as she did the other day!

Of course, defying my OCD is easier said than done. It's one thing to want to act a certain way and another to implement it. In order to help myself, I take Sertraline daily, which is the generic form of Zoloft, and plan to continue EMDR therapy. Medication aside, the treatment that's most effective for me is exposure therapy, as I did with Summer at Disneyland. It allows me to prove to myself that the intrusive thoughts I have aren't real and aren't actually going to happen. I'm learning how to calm my nervous system down on my own, although I do have Xanax on call for emergencies, like when I have a panic attack.

With this said, it's not a perfect science. There are certain things I'm not willing to give up. I still have a baby monitor in Summer's room. It gives me peace of mind, and that's okay. I've gotten better about it when I'm out of town on a work trip. I'll only check the camera once and, if she's asleep, I'll turn it off. I mean, what would I do if she woke up and I was in New York? Still, I know that sometimes when Brock is home with her, he's outside in the backyard, in the sauna, or in the garage working out, and I'm concerned he's not watching the camera. What if she sleepwalks and falls down the stairs? I feel like that's a legitimate fear, though Brock does not.

Even though he doesn't completely understand these anxieties, I will say that Brock has had a deeper appreciation of and more patience for what I struggle with ever since he attended the OCD Conference in July 2024 with me, where I received the Illumination Award from the IOCDF for my mental health advocacy.

He heard my speech, attended some seminars, and spoke to people in the OCD community, which informed and altered his perspective. Whereas, before, it made no sense to him, as he doesn't suffer from the same intrusive thoughts, now he knows that I have an actual chemical imbalance in my brain and that it's a real medical diagnosis. I don't wish it upon anyone. I'm happy that Brock isn't burdened by OCD, as it can impact many different aspects of your life. For me, parenting is just one of those areas.

Recently, my OCD presented when I did a show called *The Masked Singer* on Fox, where disguised celebrities sing songs and get voted off. I was freaking out because I had to wear a bat costume (as in the flying mammal) and perform in front of millions of viewers. I'd never worn that kind of costume, with a full headpiece, and I thought I was going to be claustrophobic, because my mother is. (My mom is also terrified of elevators and my dad is an elevator mechanic. The irony!)

Thankfully, I discovered that I don't suffer from claustrophobia, though it was hard to breathe. I had to keep telling myself I was okay and coach myself to take deep breaths. By the time I was in rehearsals onstage, I didn't even need to remove the head between takes. I faced that fear. I forced myself to be exposed to something uncomfortable. I know I can't ask any more of myself than this willingness to put myself in uncomfortable situations, so I felt very proud.

I did everything I could to prepare my voice for the show—I was steaming twice a day, and drinking tea and plenty of water. I gave up every type of carbonated beverage, alcohol, weed, even citrus and acidic foods that could cause my reflux to flare up. I even went to StretchLab so my whole body would be limber. I listened to my song on repeat and rehearsed over and over. I put in 110 percent, because I wanted to show everyone that I'm a good performer!

Sadly, I was sent home the first night, which was very disappointing, especially since I knew my second song was so much better and I was going to crush it. The truth is, I wasn't sold on that first song. It didn't play well to my voice, but I relented. And, once again, my people-pleasing tendencies bit me in the ass. When will I ever learn?! I'm sure when it airs I'll get roasted, but I don't care. I accomplished something monumental for me, even if viewers can't see it that way.

After I finished sobbing post vote-out, I reminded myself that I never would have done the show or even considered it if I hadn't been in a solid place or felt strong enough. In fact, when my team initially told me about the gig, I said, "No, absolutely not. I'm not singing on national TV again." But it was the first time I'd been offered a spot on a celebrity-driven network show. It was a big deal for me and my career, and I wasn't going to let the haters hold me back. I know that I'm not the most talented vocalist, and I'm not trying to win a Grammy. I just want to do things that bring me joy. I'm proud of myself for not being ruled by fear, for stepping out of my comfort zone, and for putting my best foot forward. These are all the things I want Summer to emulate in her own life as she grows.

In my exit interview, they asked me, "What's one thing you want the audience to know?" I looked directly into the camera and said something to the effect of "Everyone should get used to seeing me on TV, because I'm not going anywhere. I'm going to keep getting back up. I'm going to continue putting myself out there. All the people who are telling me to put the mic down, don't bother, because I'm here to stay."

When I signed on to do *Vanderpump Rules* twelve years ago, I walked in as a confident twenty-six-year-old. I stood up to the mean girls and handled my own shit. But, ultimately, season after season I got knocked down, which was a serious reality check for me (pun intended). I learned that I'm not the best at everything. I won't book every audition. I don't have the biggest following on social media. And I'm not the most liked on the show. I wish I'd been as respected as other cast members were. But I became an easy target, because I followed the rules and didn't complain. I showed up and did my job.

Gratefully, I've come to a point where I'm not crying over what people say about me. I'm resilient enough that I can read the nasty comments and then let them go. Whatever the haters say online, I know how much I brought to the show.

This became especially clear recently. I guess I'll leave you with one final spill of tea…

A few nights ago, at one of the many events the *VPR* cast gets invited to, a very polished producer of ours—who's never revealed anything in the years I've known them—finally let something slip. We were chatting about how the show started and they said, "Lisa was worried that the Disney girl who had a connection to Eddie wasn't going to participate." They were talking about me directly to my face. In other words, outing Lisa and gifting me the one thing I'd always suspected—that Lisa knew about my affair with Eddie all along. And she used it to launch *VPR*. Maybe she even suggested Brandi for season two of *The Real Housewives of Beverly Hills*, knowing about our connection and hoping it would help her land a spin-off. Who knows? Or, at the very least, once Brandi was on the show, did Lisa's wheels start turning?

The point is, I've always looked up to Lisa as a business-woman and mother figure, but I wish she had been transparent with me from the get-go. I likely still would have signed on, only with agency in that piece of my story.

On November 25, 2024, the entire existing cast of *VPR* was released and replaced, which sparked mixed emotions for me. All at once, I was surprised, relieved, and excited for the next chapter. I feel like I finally have the confidence to handle whatever comes my way. And I know there will be other shows, new projects, and exciting opportunities. I also look forward to continuing to grow my podcast and make music with the band, maybe even figure out a way to make money from my music one day! To this day, I haven't earned a penny off of "Good As Gold," aside from vinyl sales.

Early in my career I had a manager who felt more like a friend, and most of our business meetings entailed multiple martinis. He even introduced me to *his* lawyer. Looking back, it probably wasn't in my best interest to share legal representation, but I didn't know any better at the time. I just thought it was cool that I had an entertainment attorney. I vividly recall one time that he took me into a notary and said we needed to take care of something. He communicated that it was all standard, that he was looking out for my best interest, and I trusted him. Apparently one of those documents signed over the rights to "Good As Gold" to him. I don't presently have access to copies of that contract, if I ever did, and my attempts over the years to retain rights over my work or receive copies of our original contract have been unsuccessful. Maybe that will change now.

What I've realized, through this wild journey of mine, is that I don't need everyone to like me. I just want to be understood. And, in order for that to happen, I need to lean into my healing journey and face my issues head-on. I have a tendency to bury myself in distractions rather than process my trauma, and I want to encourage anyone who can relate to this to really seek the help and happiness they deserve.

I've come a long way, and I'm not stopping anytime soon. I'm embracing that all sides of me are good, from the scars to the scarlet letters, though I still prefer to be photographed on the left.

ACKNOWLEDGMENTS

Brock, I know it wasn't an easy decision to put everything about us in this book, but from the bottom of my heart, thank you for trusting me to tell *our* story here. Your encouragement has meant everything to me, and through all the ups and downs, I am so thankful we have stuck by each other. You are my rock, and I love you. I couldn't do all that I do without your support. I want you, and our life together, forever.

Mom, Dad, Cort, and Justice, you mean the world to me. I feel so blessed that you are my family. You've always been there for me, and I hope that I continue to make you proud. Even when I have kept things to myself, knowing that at any moment in time I can call you and you'll be there with zero judgment is the best feeling. You know what a challenging process this book has been for me, and I thank you for standing by me every step of the way.

Mark, I can't believe we've been on this ride together for over a decade now. Thank you for always being someone I can trust and confide in. Your belief in me gives me the confidence

I've sometimes lost. You make my life better. I genuinely don't know what I'd do without you.

Nema, who would have thought the day you came up to me at American Junkie would turn into this amazing friendship? You have been there through my lowest of lows, and I don't know how I would have gotten through such dark times without you. You are more than just my friend, you are family. I will always be grateful for you and never want to do life without you.

Kevin and Lando (the 27s), you came into my life at the craziest time and when I needed you the most. You helped me get my mojo back by getting me in the studio and reminding me why I love performing so much. "Apples" will forever be a banger. I can't wait to see what we do next!

Emily, what a journey this book has been. There were so many points when I wanted to give up, but you got me to the finish line. I love what we have created together. Thank you for your diligence and hard work in bringing this dream of mine to life!

To Jacqui and everyone at Hachette and Grand Central Publishing, from the bottom of my heart, thank you for believing in me and championing my story. I knew the second I walked out of the meeting that this was the home for my book. I can now check off a major box on my career bucket list because of *you*!

To Tess at Europa Content and Justin and Katie at IAG, you believed in this project before the pen hit the paper. Thank you for helping bring this book to life! There were so many hurdles we had to overcome to get here, and I couldn't have navigated this journey without your steady hand.

Daniela, the most badass attorney there ever was. You have been the most incredible addition to my team, and I can't wait to see what else we do together.

Alex Baskin, Jeremiah Smith, Kurt Murphy, and every single person at Evolution Media, thank you for never giving up on me. Creating magic on the screen with y'all has been one of the highlights of my life.

Andy Cohen and the entire Bravo Network and NBCU family, I can't believe we made it eleven seasons together. Every reunion, *WWHL,* and BravoCon we've done together have been some of my favorite experiences and moments in my adult life. I hope to have many more!

To the cast of *Vanderpump Rules,* what a time! Through all the chaos, we have made so many memories together. I hope you know how much you all mean to me.

To my Amat girls, Natalie B, Kelli, Janet, and all my other friends and family who have stood by my side from day one, you're the real ones. I will never forget what you've done for me and the integral roles you have each played in my journey.

To the fans, I could not do what I do without your support. Hearing all your stories and how you've related to mine has truly been life-changing. Thank you for being on this journey with me, and know that it's not over yet! You will never know how much you all mean to me. Your words of encouragement fuel my spirit and keep me feeling good as gold!

And, most important, to my daughter, Summer Moon: If you read this one day, I hope you know that putting myself fully out there has never been easy, but I know I'm doing the right thing because I have seen the good that has come from sharing my story. I hope I always make you proud and never embarrass you… too much. Everything I do is for you. Thank you for making me a mother. I feel like the luckiest woman on this earth because I get to be *your* mom. Your love keeps me going every single day.

ABOUT THE AUTHOR

Scheana Shay is an actress, host, and television personality from the Emmy-nominated Bravo TV series *Vanderpump Rules*. Other notable television credits include roles on popular shows such as *Lopez vs Lopez, 90210, Greek, Victorious,* and *Jonas*. The Southern California native is also the host of the award-winning podcast *Scheananigans*. Scheana currently resides in Los Angeles with her husband Brock and daughter Summer Moon.

@scheana on all platforms